Donated by Green Beans Coffee
cupofjoeforajoe.com

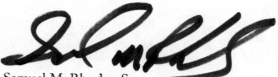

Samuel M. Rhodes, Sr.
President/CEO Warrior Outreach, Inc.
Command Sergeant Major (Retired)
U.S. Army Cell 706-505-0708
sam@warrioroutreach.org
For more information on our effort to Partner to help, please visit our
website at http://www.warrioroutreach.org/.

1 June 2018

Breaking the Chains of Stigma Associated With Post Traumatic Stress

BREAKING THE CHAINS OF STIGMA ASSOCIATED WITH POST TRAUMATIC STRESS

SAM M. RHODES

authorHOUSE®

AuthorHouse™ LLC
1663 Liberty Drive
Bloomington, IN 47403
www.authorhouse.com
Phone: 1-800-839-8640

Published by AuthorHouse   02/10/2014

ISBN: 978-1-4918-4979-8 (sc)
ISBN: 978-1-4918-4978-1 (hc)
ISBN: 978-1-4918-4977-4 (e)

Library of Congress Control Number: 2014900239

Any people depicted in stock imagery provided by Thinkstock are models,
and such images are being used for illustrative purposes only.
Certain stock imagery © Thinkstock.

This book is printed on acid-free paper.

Because of the dynamic nature of the Internet, any web addresses or links contained in
this book may have changed since publication and may no longer be valid. The views
expressed in this work are solely those of the author and do not necessarily reflect the views
of the publisher, and the publisher hereby disclaims any responsibility for them.

TABLE OF CONTENTS

FOREWORD

Within the first month of entering the job of Army Chief of Staff in April, 2007, I saw two studies about the health of an Army that had been at war for five and one-half years. The first study, our annual personnel survey, said that 90% of those surveyed across the Army would **not** be willing to get assistance for a behavioral health issue because they felt that doing so would impact their careers. The second, a study on the impacts of post-traumatic stress and traumatic brain injury, said that the Army should expect 10-12% of our deployed Soldiers to be diagnosed with some form of PTS after their first deployment. The study indicated that, with subsequent deployments, the percentage of those affected would increase to 15-17% on the second deployment and to 17-20% on the third.

In the spring of 2007, we were just starting the surge, so at that time, I was expecting 5-10 more years of continued deployments. When I did the math, I saw that I would have fewer and fewer troops available to deploy, and I realized that such a situation could pose a significant problem for the Army and for the country.

It was clear that if we were going to provide our Soldiers with the care they needed to recover from war, we had to begin by defeating the stigma surrounding behavioral health. I also realized that to have an impact, we were going to have to change deeply embedded service culture—a culture that values toughness and that encourages Soldiers to never quit or accept defeat. This proved to be a tall order, and that summer, we began an Army-wide program to educate our Soldiers and leaders in the science of post-traumatic stress and traumatic brain injury.

We also looked for institutional biases. For example, on the application for a security clearance, we found a question that asked if the applicant had ever sought mental health care—a significant impediment to reducing stigma!

I met Command Sergeant Major Sam Rhodes as we began our efforts. One of my first visits to an Army installation in the spring of 2007 was to Fort Benning, Georgia, the home of the Army's infantry—the toughest of the tough. During my visit, I was given a copy of the post newspaper, *The Bayonet*, which had an article in it by CSM Rhodes discussing the challenges he faced in dealing with post-traumatic stress. Given where we were as an Army at that time, I was immediately impressed by the courage it took to write the article and asked to meet Sam.

When we met, Sam shared his own story with me and explained his growing passion to help other Soldiers suffering from post-traumatic stress. I encouraged him to expand his efforts, and we kept in touch after he retired. He shared with me the feedback he received from Soldiers and their families after they had heard his presentations, and he gave me a copy of his first book, *Changing the Military Culture of Silence*. I could only be impressed as he carried his message across the country.

I have seen first-hand Sam's commitment to Soldiers and their families, to removing the barriers to care for our Soldiers and veterans, and to extending a hand to the men and women of our society suffering from post-traumatic stress. *Breaking the Chains of Stigma* reflects his personal journey and experiences with post-traumatic stress. His mantra is, "One doesn't experience life without experiencing life-changing events. It's how you handle those events that counts." That's great advice for everyone.

We all need to work on reducing the stigma attached to behavioral health care—in society as well as in the military—but that is a daunting

INTRODUCTION

Concerned Moms

Hello Mr. Rhodes, I have been thinking about emailing you, but I did not want to be a bother or seem like a hysterical mom. This whole experience since my son came home from Afghanistan has been horrible. I watched the HBO series <u>War Torn</u>, *and one mother in it said that it is as if they took her son, sent him back shredded up, and now she has to try to put the pieces back together.*

My son is being treated for PTS and he is in the Army Substance Abuse Program. He was 1 of 20 picked from his unit to go into the most volatile part of Afghanistan on missions. I am not a veteran, so I do not know the terms, but obviously you know how it works when the highest scoring ones are picked. My son was always with the sergeants when they met with the AMP's—he was right there always with the sergeants. He was very popular and at the top of his unit.

We went early to greet him before his unit's homecoming, but it was postponed for a few more days. The Commander was back, though, because he had to attend a ceremony at the White House. As a result, the families got a briefing from him later on when he returned. After this meeting, my husband introduced himself and said that we needed to talk to our son because he had been sent to an area in Afghanistan where there was a large concentration of the enemy. This was news to me because I never knew he was in the dangerous parts of Afghanistan. My son had told me where he was, and very naively I would look at that area on the map, watch news reports about other areas, and think, "Oh thank God he is not there." Well I found out he was in the bad parts. I had had no idea.

    We learned that our son had been screened for PTS and put on medication for it. He began crying hysterically and was put on more medicine. Then he was sent to Poplar Springs in Virginia for a month's stay. He did not expect to be ostracized when he got back. His whole unit changed positions, the sergeants that he had deployed with were sent to other units and new ones were brought in. He had a new lieutenant who publicly humiliated him in front of a class he was teaching. They really do not know him, nor did they care. He was doing fine. He would tell his counselor that they were not going to break him; he was going to be the example of something positive.

    Then he went back and after about a week, he said, "They broke me."
    He tried to talk to his commander, simply stating that everyone had changed since deployment. He really got into trouble for saying that he wanted to go to JAG.

    He was told, "What do you think you are, a barracks lawyer?"
    He was just recently asked by a sergeant what he would do and say if he put a loaded gun to his head.

    My son said, "Pull the trigger."

    Right after that he was told, "There is something wrong with you."
    After this he was told to go and stand outside. How can any Soldier treat another Soldier like that, especially one that they know is being treated for PTS? That is just wrong. He was given a profile from the doctor to have limited hours, and they have ignored that. The doctor said that he should not go to any ranges, and they have ignored that, too. He was at the ranges with the sounds that bring on flashbacks. He is reduced to an empty Soldier, just basically going through the motions of the day. He cannot go on jumps, he cannot carry a weapon, and he cannot work the roads. Now the Commander is putting him in for separation and an article hearing where he will be reduced to PFC. This would not be happening if he had not gone for PTS treatment. He graduated from basic training in the AMP's program, he was awarded "Soldier of the Quarter" while in Afghanistan, and he got a perfect score. He lost three of his friends in Afghanistan. He had always been an outstanding Soldier until being in combat and having to kill people. He has been abandoned by every one of the sergeants in his unit.

Earlier that morning, I had awakened from one of the worst dreams I had ever had. It wasn't really a dream, though—I was there! I was experiencing the after-effects of losing two great company commanders and watching their bodies being placed into bags. I knew then that I should go for counseling.

Although I had not developed substance abuse issues, I did gain weight and was up to 260 pounds. In spite of the weight gain, I was remarkably fit and able to run better than most. However, I found myself not feeling very well, and I consulted a primary physician assistant who sent me to the hospital to have some lab work done. Early the next morning I received a phone call from the TMC (Troup Medical Clinic). The caller sounded a little anxious.

She said, "CSM, you need to come to the TMC right now."
I replied, "I am in a meeting."
She said, "CSM, don't make me come get you."
I went into the physician assistant's office, and he told me that my lab work showed signs of heart disease. He said that if I didn't do something about it soon, he couldn't predict a timeline for me. We talked about the findings and about my family history. My father and his brother had both passed away at the ages of 64 and 65 from heart disease, so my family history was not encouraging. After contemplating all this information, as well as learning of my booming blood pressure, I took a hard look in the mirror. I decided to receive counseling, via the telephone, from a combat stress doctor at Walter Reed Medical Center. I had been counseled by this same doctor in Iraq during my last deployment. I started dieting and working out harder and harder. The TMC folks continued to stay on top of my progress, monitoring my daily blood pressure checks and monthly lab work. During this period I learned that the root causes of all my issues were the anxiety and emotional instability that I had been dealing with since my extended stay in the Middle East.

Though we, as leaders, choose to fight most of our individual battles by ourselves, it's comforting to know we have excellent medical personnel who care about Soldiers of all ranks. We definitely don't appreciate them enough! Ms. Wilbanks told me that leaders can be helpful to their Soldiers by being aware of the symptoms of PTS and making it a priority to get training and assistance for each Soldier who needed help. I believe my personal experiences have made me more sensitive to helping my Soldiers. Over the years, I have at times made light of that fact, saying, "I thank God for the ACUs" which covered up all the additional pounds that I had gained because of my anxiety. Those uniforms had room for my growth, and although I am sure that others noticed my weight gain, they were kind about it.

My weight issue was corrected through continued dedication and with the help of the medical staff at TMC 5. I began working out twice a day, mostly running and going to the gym. Spending a lot of extra time working out made a really big difference for me. Not only did I gain a lot of energy, but also I truly believe that the extra effort to achieve fitness helped me control some of the mental challenges that I had to deal with when I returned. That first summer back home, after three years of deployment, was a tough one for me. For 30 months, the battle rhythm of combat had kept me focused and engaged. To say I had felt at home in Iraq would not have been far from the truth. It was hard to feel the same way when I first came back.

After six months of extensive working out, I had lost more than 40 pounds and could run like the wind again. As a result, physically, I felt and continue to feel terrific. Emotionally, I have recovered to a certain degree. However, I still have issues whenever someone mentions a Soldier's death. For example, who would have thought a Soldier could have a Post Traumatic Stress incident while running down the road in a garrison environment? I was running down Moye Road at about 5:45 AM when, all of a sudden, three loud bursts of gunfire rang out. My heart felt as if it had stopped on the first burst. Then there was a second burst and then the third. My eyes began to water—I knew instantly what the reason was for those three volleys. It was a firing squad from the 1st Battalion, 50th Infantry, rehearsing for a funeral support mission. I tried to continue running, but I was remembering that time and time again this had happened to me over the past four years.

Post Traumatic Stress, in my opinion, is not curable in my case and will remain a part of my life forever. I am dealing with it by trying to replace bad memories with the great memories of those fallen comrades whose efforts have protected our American way of life. We, as leaders, have not been trained to handle our reactions to losing our Soldiers or even losing our fellow leaders during combat. We continue to learn and grow through the struggles of our current conflict. It's an instinct to be a warrior. It's also an instinct to be saddened by the recurring memories of the loss of those great Americans. I am not able to develop an instinct to force these memories to disappear. Ms. Wilbanks emphasized that when these memories interfere with normal functioning or result in thoughts of suicide, we must get help immediately.

With that warning in mind, when I attended a 47th Infantry Regiment's reunion, I talked to some of the heroes who had fought in previous wars. I talked to them specifically about what I was feeling and going through on a daily basis.

The best words I heard were, "Never forget, but let it go."
I would add, "Never forget, **get help**, and let it go."

CHAPTER 2

Stigma—A Returning Soldier's Worst Enemy

STIGMA—A sign of social unacceptability: the shame or disgrace attached to something regarded as socially unacceptable (Encarta World English Dictionary).

What is this really saying? In my opinion, stigma is nothing more than fear of the unknown, as it relates to Post Traumatic Stress (PTS). Leaders and family members are challenged because they don't know enough about PTS. They fear those who have it, they do not understand it, and they may place a stigma upon those who have it. Leaders may live in fear of developing it themselves. We who suffer from it believe we are closer to being normal and honest than those who say of their war experience, "It didn't affect me at all." As Soldiers, veterans and leaders, we are supposed to be strong, brave and true. Fear is something the enemy feels toward us. We run *to* the fight—not *from* it. But in reality, we *do* have fear. Fear of letting our team down. Fear of not measuring up. I remember asking the commander from my brigade in Iraq to allow us to remove our combat gear on the Forward Operating Base. When he refused, I explained to him my thoughts that the enemy was looking at us and saying, "We have them on the run; they're scared." About half way through the tour, we took off our gear, and the enemy realized we were no longer afraid of them. One day a month, they attacked us with mortars to see if we would go back into our shell. I believe this conduct made us stronger. Similarly, I think that those who have PTS will become stronger when society recognizes that they are normal and welcomes them to come out of the shadows.

As leaders, we have to demonstrate the art of leadership (the ability to influence Soldiers to accomplish a mission, no matter how dangerous). As I traveled across America and spoke to Soldiers, families, leaders, veterans and staff members of the Veterans Administration, I was asked the same question over and over again:

"How did you feel when you started openly talking about your struggles with Post Traumatic Stress? Were you afraid of what your fellow Command Sergeant Majors thought of you?"

The answer is "Yes." But over the last seven years, I've learned to control that fear. In 2005 and 2006 I kept those fears close to my chest. Only my therapist and a few close friends knew of my struggles. However, in April, 2007, I had to speak out. I had to get additional help after thoughts of suicide started flooding my mind. Initially, I felt anxiety, depression and extreme emotional stress after a magazine article I wrote about PTS was published in a military publication. Some days I would be resilient and accept the idea that tomorrow would be better. The friends that were true friends accepted me and helped me develop coping skills. However, there were others who couldn't or wouldn't acknowledge that I needed help. They shunned me. It's hard to accept being one person going into a war, and being a stranger to yourself coming out of that war. The sights, sounds, smells and feel of war change an individual. Those leaders who shunned me are now my friends. I don't have any hatred or any ill feelings toward them. PTS, with its stigma, and TBI (Traumatic Brain Injury) involve a learning curve. People must come to accept the fact that when Soldiers have survived very tough parts of life, they need time to adjust to normal conditions. We almost need to do as we did when we sent Soldiers to Germany. At that time, we created a Head Start program to teach them the basics of the German language to facilitate their adapting to the society they were visiting. Why don't we create a crash course on life after war? We could learn how to help a fellow warrior adapt to normal life again by recognizing signs and symptoms and learning a skill set to assist him in the adaptation process every day. We could teach him resilience.

CHAPTER 3

Using Resilience and Support
to Fight Suicide

I have gained strength through building resilience. However, in spite of great family and community support, I still face challenges every day. No other person can know exactly what I am thinking or how I may react to those thoughts. I must always be my own first line of defense, but it is important to have a good listener who understands my needs.

My 32-mile commute to work at Ft. Benning offers a lot of time for my mind to wander. One morning, after a tough night of really bad dreams, I was thinking about the loss of so many Soldiers who had served with me. I kept wondering why I had survived when so many others had not. I was trying to focus on the future and struggling to understand why I was having so much difficulty adjusting. The constant pain inside me seemed endless. It was the everyday anxiety that many warriors of past and present wars continue to struggle with, whether they admit it or not. When placed into uncomfortable situations, I frequently became nauseated and made numerous trips to the bathroom. I often thought about taking my own life. Just as I was thinking about how my life had changed since January of 2008 when Cathy and I married, the blue tooth phone in my truck rang.

I heard Cathy's voice saying, "Are you okay? You didn't look so good this morning." They were not the words one wants to hear from his wife.

Her next words were, "I love you. It'll be okay. We will handle it."

Those were comforting words coming from a very giving person. Cathy has blessed my life, reaching out to me and helping to lift me from the bottom of the barrel of my life's struggles. Before 2008, I had felt alone and helpless. I had gone through a divorce and battles with PTS and suicide. When I met Cathy, she embraced me for who I am, not for what I was suffering. I spent many months prior to our marriage trying to figure out why she loved me in spite of the fact that I had so much baggage and so little to offer her.

When changes occurred in my life, Cathy and I tried to handle them by dealing with one at a time, but the anxiety and depression continued. Although I was surrounded by a wonderful wife and a daughter who seemed to accept everything about me, I still wondered if my life would be another survivor story or the story of the last straw that broke the warrior's back. Seeing horrific injuries and death torments the soul, and there is always a battle after one has come close to taking his/her own life. I believe I am more vulnerable now than when I first considered it. My research shows that 30% of those who try to take their own lives eventually succeed. I don't want to be in that group. We American Soldiers, veterans, fathers, sons, and friends need to embrace those that want to support us. Had I not spoken out, I probably would be a statistic today. I could have been one of the many Soldiers who have taken their own lives. I am sure that coming out and speaking openly about my struggles with Post Traumatic Stress and suicidal thoughts saved my life.

Quite often these days, I attend funerals of Soldiers killed in combat or, sadly, killed by their own hands. When we lose a brave Soldier in combat, we honor his memory with flags and ceremonies. When we lose a Soldier to suicide, we ask why. Those who suffer with PTS know why. The haunting despair that never stops lurking around the dark corners of the mind finally pulled the trigger. Post Traumatic Stress distorts reality. It makes life cheap. It is a death trap unless you get help. Suicide in the military is on the increase. I believe that stigma is at the heart of that problem. We need to help others to understand our illness and remove its stigma, and we must be brave enough to ask for help.

CHAPTER 4

Compassionate Leadership

I support the ideas of an Army officer who spoke to me about his ongoing battle with PTS. Like many of us, he second guesses himself about some of the decisions he made during the war—decisions that cost lives. Our Army focuses on inspirational leadership, which is the heart of the Army. This remarkable officer informed me that, although being an inspirational leader is good, we need an Army of leaders who provide compassion along with inspiration. While traveling the country speaking about PTS and resilience, I've heard a lot of truly amazing stories about bravery, loss, and second guessing. Soldiers are human; they sometimes make mistakes. They need to feel that, regardless of their mistakes, their lives are much more important than any mistake. Leaders must display compassion in order for their Soldiers to feel inspired and know that their leaders care and will listen to them.

CHAPTER 5

Returning from War; a New Army Directive

During the Vietnam era and before, Soldiers came home and were spat upon and called "baby killers." Now, forty years later, all we hear is "Thanks for your service." After those few words, it is as if you don't exist anymore. People feel they have done their duty and said thanks, but what about me as a person? I'm more than just a uniform. I can take the uniform off, but I can't erase the memories. I look at those people as they ask me questions, and I wonder if they are just ignorant. I am tired of hearing, "Thanks for your service, thanks for what you do, and welcome home." All of these words won't begin to give back what was taken from all of us in combat. People smile, wave, and show appreciation, never fully understanding just why they're doing so. Sometimes I don't even know why they are. As an example, I was driving through a major city just a few weeks ago when I saw a flag flying on Memorial Day. The flag was torn and ripped but still flying. I could see that they were patriotic, but it was time for a new flag. They keep trying though. I came home from combat to balloons and a big sign that said, "Welcome Home, Hero." During the party that followed, I celebrated, hugged, and began a new life.

But I wondered to myself, "Did I get a welcome home or was this a memorial service of a different kind . . . a Welcome Home Memorial?"

Yes, that's what I think happened to a lot of us. Those of us who didn't get a Purple Heart for visual wounds received a welcome home sign and a bunch of hugs. Then we moved on. Or did we? I have tried and tried over the past six years to move forward with my life. I even managed to hide my problems from society for many months. Then I could do so no longer. In April, 2007, I wrote an article entitled "Post Traumatic Stress Impacts All Levels of Leadership" that was published in the Infantry magazine, *Professional Forum*. What I didn't know then and, therefore, did not include in that article was that the military leadership of our country had been ordered not to place a stigma on any Soldier who returns from combat with PTS. I know now that leaders have been instructed that PTS cannot be used as a reason to disqualify such a Soldier for a security clearance. WOW, we have come a long way, haven't we? The Chief of Staff of the Army issued guidance stating that the Army would put a "full court press" on helping Soldiers with PTS. General George W. Casey recognized the impact of stigma on the force and issued that order. As a result, an unknown number of lives have been saved. We have come a long way, but we still have a long way to go. Will we now be observing, reporting, and discussing? That simply isn't enough to help our nation's veterans—current, past and future.

I was both excited and distressed with the directive from the Chief of Staff of the Army, knowing the intent of his message and also living through the conditions it describes. In 2008, I traveled to Hawaii for a long overdue vacation and an opportunity to talk to some WW II and Vietnam veterans, as well as some 25th ID Soldiers who had just returned from Iraq. As happy as I was to meet Soldiers who were excited about having a CSM of my caliber talking to them, I was equally distressed to learn that their chain of command was ignoring the Army's directive to stop associating a stigma to their desire to get mental health counseling.

To a man, they all said the same thing: "My supervisor asked me this morning, 'What is your Mental Health Administration appointment for? What the hell is wrong with you?'"

These Soldiers felt that either their supervisors didn't care or they had no idea what the Chief of Staff had said to his staff and the leadership of this country. As I looked at these heroes, I saw what I see in the mirror every morning—stress, despair and confusion. When I travel across this country, I hear the same story over and over again at every installation.

CHAPTER 6

Struggling with PTS and Its Stigma

I've talked to numerous therapists about my struggles with PTS and how it affects my every waking moment. Even in April, 2008, when I very reluctantly put in my military retirement request, I was afraid—afraid of the future and what it had to offer me. I was directed by the Veterans Administration to go to another psychiatric brain surgeon in Columbus, GA. I assumed that meant that the ones at Fort Benning were lacking something. The real story is that they weren't lacking anything. The doctors wanted a third, fourth and a fifth opinion.

As I sat in the doctor's office and waited, I watched young kids who were getting counseling for a variety of conditions. Several veterans were there, too. Finally, I got to see the doctor.

He said, "Tell me about your combat experiences."

I was shocked, not sure what he wanted to know. As he looked at me, I was thinking, "Man, that's original! For over four years I have been suffering from a newly identified disease and not one counselor has taken the time to ask me that question." (Instead, I would get questions about what had been happening to me during the week, and what I thought was causing such experiences.) Impressed with this new approach, I started to explain the anxiety of war and the trauma of losing fellow Soldiers and seeing suffering

Iraqis. I told the doctor that I had grown to love and appreciate the Iraqis so much that I sponsored a family so that they could come to the United States. I confessed that I had suffered mixed emotions after my first fifteen months of combat—so much so that I figured out a way to return to the war, only one month after leaving. Then, dramatically, three months into that assignment, I was selected to be the Command Sergeant Major for an organization that would be deploying again, and I took that assignment as well. Several months into that tour, immediately following the death of two snipers assigned to my unit, my problems began. I explained that now I was trying to help others, and that doing so actually helped me because I felt I was giving something back. The doctor shared with me details about some senior officers who had been visiting him to get private treatment since the war began. I was surprised at his words. Was it really possible that the biggest fear senior officers have is that of developing PTS? Are they afraid of the stigma?

Is PTS contagious? No. It's not like HIV. You can't get it from a dirty needle. Is that what's wrong with our society? Are people afraid that if they shake the hand of a service member who suffers from PTS, they might get the same disease? Yes, I believe some people think that way, and I feel bad about that. People are placing a stigma on this illness. However, I feel better knowing that many service members are going to get treatment and are being helped by doctors. This is the way we have to tackle this disease—head on.

My own struggles continued in the fall of 2008. I vividly remember that as I was heading off to work one day, I stopped to watch the morning news. The feature was a story out of Fort Bragg, NC, about people giving a newly built home to a young Soldier who had lost both legs. My eyes started to water.

As I left, I turned to Cathy, my wife, and said," See you after work, Babe. I love you."

While I was driving the 30 minute commute to my office at Fort Benning, my mind flashed back to the many memorial services for fallen Soldiers I had attended. All the feelings of guilt that I had previously felt returned. The memories came fast and painfully—CPT Harding, who died without seeing his newborn child, the 19 year-old kid who never got to see his twentieth birthday, the son whose dad was killed just down the road from his Forward Operating Base, and the warrant officer who had retired from the Army and come back to Iraq as a civilian contractor, only to die in an IED attack. Tears streamed down my face. The guilt and anguish became uncontrollable. I knew what I needed to do. I knew that it was too early in the day to call my doctor. So I did one better. I called #1 (my wife) on my speed dial. The phone rang and a loving voice answered. I choked up and tearfully said, "I love you, Babe."

Her wonderful voice began to console me, "What's wrong, why are you crying?"

I told her what had happened and explained to her my guilt and my anger at not having any wounds to show the world . . . the anger of not losing a leg for folks to acknowledge. I told her that I wished I had lost both my legs.

She said, "That would have been fine. I would have loved you with no legs."

I was amazed and overjoyed to hear her say, "Babe, it's okay to cry. You're a wonderful, caring person; it's your nature."

I told her good bye and finished my drive to work. This comforting conversation reminded me that there is nothing better than waking up to someone holding you after you just had the worse nightmare of your life!! More blessings than you can imagine come because of sharing and getting the ones you dearly love involved in your healing. It won't reduce the pain in your heart—it won't reduce the anxiety and stress—it will simply make you feel that you're not alone. We must destroy the stigma placed on our veterans and service members, so they will feel free to confide in their loved ones and find hope for a better future.

CHAPTER 7

Struggling through the Transition to Civilian Life

I retired on December 31, 2008, having battled through the challenges of war and having served my country for almost 30 years. It was time. The transition for those suffering mental health problems isn't easy. Most would say that if one tells folks he has PTS or even mentions that at one time he had been diagnosed with it, it's a given that he's not going to get a job. It's become so difficult, that many Soldiers and veterans will lie on their resumes rather than try to decide whether a certain employer is a veteran supporter or just another agency protecting its ass.

Although I do not think I will ever be cured of PTS, General Rhonda Cornum, whom I proudly refer to in another part of this book, has expressed a scientific opinion that holds out much hope for not only improvement, but also for the cure of others:

"According to the National Institutes of Mental Health (NIMH), PTSD is a symptom-driven diagnosis, a particular variety of anxiety disorder[1]. Information from the Veteran's Administration's National Center for PTSD shows that many individuals become free of their symptoms and maintain

---

[1] http://www.nimh.nih.gov/health/publications/post-traumatic-stress-disorder-ptsd/index.shtml.

that symptom-free state for the rest of their lives[2]. Given that PTSD is defined by symptoms, having none would have to be considered "cured." Unfortunately, in Sam's particular case, he may never achieve "symptom-free" status; certainly he does not think he will. In this way, PTSD is like many other disorders: when evidence-based treatments are applied, some people respond with a "cure," some have reduction in their symptoms, and some people just do not respond. But in a population of people with the disorder, certainly more will improve with treatment than without it! Of course, the first step in the road to recovery is admitting the problem is there. Sam Rhodes describes one man's journey, documents roadblocks that may not exist for many other disorders, and offers valuable suggestions for reducing those roadblocks."

Rhonda Cornum, Ph.D. M.D.
Brigadier General, United States Army (Retired)

Certainly the last three years of my life have been better because of my developing resilience and adding structure, activity, and support to my lifestyle. Yes, it's really that simple. Place some structure in your life, and get involved with activities and your community. Actively seek support, visit with friends, talk with those around you and accept the idea that you're not alone. It's hard not to feel ashamed, even though it is so rewarding to have served your country and defended this nation at its time of need. Finally, be sure to share your concerns and feelings with your family, friends and those who genuinely care about you. You know who they are. They're the people who will listen to what's happening in your life. The psychiatrists are great. But the real help you need comes from those you love and trust.

As I transitioned from the Army to civilian life, I felt as though there was a stigma on me. I submitted a resume for an announced position through CPOL. After going through the gauntlet and finally getting selected to be considered, I was given an interview. As most

---

2   http://www.ptsd.va.gov/public/treatment/therapy-med/treatment-ptsd.asp.

of us with PTS do, I became excited and anxious. I introduced myself to the interviewer.

Before I could say anything whatsoever, he said, "I read your article in *Infantry Magazine* about your battle with PTS. It is a very good article."

Instead of asking me questions about my background or qualifications, he asked me how I was doing. I paused, took a deep breath and said, "Sir, I am doing fine."

I spoke confidently, yet with a bit of confusion. I replied that I was doing as well as anyone who had spent 30 out of 32 months in combat could do. I explained that, although I had done everything possible to ensure that my Soldiers and I would survive, the Soldiers that never returned home weighed heavily on my heart. I reminded him that it is not honest for anyone who returns from the Iraq or Afghanistan battlefield to say, "I am good; it didn't affect me." I have talked to thousands and thousands of troops, civilians and veterans over the past few years. More and more of them are opening up. It hurts to acknowledge our illness, but we have to be resilient, look up, and expect tomorrow to be a better day.

A friend of mine once said, "Today is tomorrow's yesterday."

He is right. Keep looking toward a better tomorrow, a tomorrow full of hope.

After that interview, I got a short email saying, "Thanks for applying. You were not selected for the position."

It was amazing just how much my life had changed following the release of the article I had written for the Infantry magazine. For me, that article was the first step in breaking the chains of stigma that held me down. It chronicled my personal battle with life after my diagnosis of PTS. Soon after it was published, many leaders at Fort Benning surrounded me with much needed support. I had been to the river; I had been to the place where most warriors and veterans go when life seems to be worthless to them. I had nearly reached that point in late March, and I finally reached my lowest point early in April, 2007. Although I now knew more about PTS, the nightmares and flashbacks never went away. Every part of my life and support seemed empty. The constant reminders of the deaths of five Soldiers during my last tour in Iraq had left me questioning whether I was a leader or a failure. I finally accepted the fact that I had done all that I could have done as a leader.

After I was diagnosed with PTS, believe it or not, I was somewhat relieved. Now I knew, to some extent, what was wrong with me and that I was not alone. Now I knew the name of my problem. I read every article I could find about PTS. I learned that Audie Murphy, America's most decorated hero from World War II, had suffered from PTS. At that time it was called by different names—battle fatigue or shell shock. **Audie Leon Murphy (June 20, 1925-May 28, 1971), the most decorated American Soldier of World War II, suffered from Post Traumatic Stress after his return from the war. He was reportedly plagued by insomnia, bouts of depression, and nightmares related to his numerous battles. In an effort to draw attention to the problems of returning Korean and Vietnam War veterans, Murphy spoke out candidly about his own problems with PTS.**

CHAPTER 8

The Effects of the Deaths of my Soldiers

For over two years, I worked for Lockheed Martin as a Project Manager. I was fortunate to have their untiring support of my occasional visits to our troops at various locations. I believed it was necessary for me to tell them the importance of hanging in there and never giving up.

One late afternoon in 2010, I was in my office after giving a presentation. As a former Brigade Command Sergeant Major for the 192nd Infantry Brigade, I normally received several phone calls and emails following such events. One call came from my former Personal Security NCO, a staff sergeant whom I grew to love like a son. We had served together during my last tour.

Out of the blue, he said, "CSM, I was wondering if I could discuss something with you."

He then told me that he had received a call from some of his friends in the battalion whom I had addressed. They were wondering if my PSD NCO thought that I had been "looking to die in Iraq."

He said, "Sergeant Major, I have often asked myself that question. I know that you took special precautions to not place any Soldier on the security team in any situation that you didn't find necessary. You went as far as checking IED holes and checking the five and 25 meter areas around vehicles for IEDs before allowing us to get out of our vehicles. I also noticed that when we lost the first five Soldiers in April, their deaths changed you. You seemed to gain energy, staying up late at Battle X-Ray, asking questions about when the last patrol was coming back, and actively doing more patrols. You were relentless in pre-combat checks before going on a mission."

That comment surprised me, but it really shouldn't have; my goal had been to have everyone return home, and return in one piece. Although I had never lost a son or daughter in combat, I still felt great pain when I lost Soldiers whose family was waiting for their safe return. I had returned to Iraq on short notice for my final tour, believing that I could make a difference. My expectations were met during my first 100 days in Iraq. The Squadron Commander, LTC Bill Simril, and I observed many positives in a very dangerous sector. However, it all hit home on that one day in April, 2005, when we received the first call that two of our Soldiers were being evacuated. After several days, one died and then the other. The memorial service was tough on the unit, but even tougher on me as it ripped my heart apart. These two young men had departed life way too early. The nights immediately following the notification of their deaths became a great challenge to me. I found myself not sleeping much and sometimes sleepwalking. I barricaded my door to prevent any sleepwalking issues. A few days later another Soldier died, and then two great company commanders were killed. This left the unit heartbroken. As I arrived at the scene where their lives were taken by an insurgent IED, my heart seemed to stop. I began to shake, and my eyes filled with tears when I saw the unbelievable carnage. The first responders to the incident were frantic, to say the least, each of them trying to be professional and strong. I knew this was a critical junction in the unit's combat tour. I had to hold back. I had to be strong. I couldn't allow them to see me cry. I had to keep the unit together.

One medic, a really wonderful kid trying to do his job as a Mortuary Affairs Specialist, was trying to police up the remains—legs, arms, etc.

He walked up to me with the hand of one of the Soldiers and said, "Sergeant Major, what do you want me to do with this?"

I reached out my hand and took the wedding band off the severed hand and told him to put the hand with the body along with the other personal effects. This was probably the most challenging day I had ever had. I would have sacrificed myself if it could have brought them back to life. On many occasions after that, I left the Forward Operating Base

(FOB) without concern for my own life; only praying that if one of us had to not return, it would be me.

After reflecting on those events, I never gave my PSD NCO a direct answer to his question. I just simply told him that my life was no more valuable than that of any of our men and women who have died in war.

CHAPTER 9

My Combat Support Hospital Flight

The observations that the staff sergeant had made in 2005 and questioned me about in 2010 were valid ones. Something apparently was not right with me.

In June of 2005, I was air lifted to Baghdad Combat Support Hospital after being found unconscious in an area of the FOB. All I remember is that I was walking around one day, and then the next thing I can recall is this young female sergeant on the helicopter placing a piece of paper in the pocket of my uniform. When I finally regained some understanding of what was going on, I was in the hospital with everyone standing around me. Later on that day I remember that the doctor told me that I was going to be air lifted to Landstul Hospital in Germany in the morning. When he left the room and I thought about my options, I wondered what I was going to do. I asked the nurse if I could use the phone to let my unit know what was going on. When she consented, I contacted my unit's personal security team. I told them to come to the hospital with my gear and weapon at 0800 the next day to pick me up. I said, "I am being released back to the unit." I stretched the truth, but it was the truth, as I saw it. That night I informed the nurse that I was not going anywhere except back to my troops. She informed the doctor. That next morning the first person I saw was the Squadron Commander, Colonel Bill Simril.

I told him, "Sir, I'm ready to go." After he had a long talk with the medical folks, we were on our way back to my unit.

As soon as I reached my unit, First Sergeant Renteria, who had found me and with the help of some other Soldiers had taken me to the medics, welcomed me back.

He said, "I found you unconscious, lying on the ground. You need to take it easy. You've been at this for a long time, and we need you."

It was then I realized I needed to get help. I had talked before to the Combat Stress Team about other Soldiers, and I had used their advice to help others. This was different. I needed help myself. I started seeing the Combat Stress folks on a regular basis, doing some exercises and generally just trying to slow the pace down a little. However, as we continued to take casualties, each one seemed to hurt more than the one before.

CHAPTER 10

A Perfect Situation

In August, 2005, COL Charles Durr, the Brigade Commander, offered me a job at Fort Benning to be the Basic Combat Training Brigade CSM. I informed him that I would love to return to Georgia and to serve especially in this type of unit where I felt I could make a difference.

He asked the critical question, "What do you see yourself doing in three years?"

I answered, "Sir, I want to do something to help Soldiers."

I informed him that if I were selected, it would be December, 2005, or January, 2006, before I could report. About a month passed before I got my second 0230 hour call letting me know I had been selected for this great position. As we talked we both agreed that the position would wait for me to return. In late November, 2005, the Squadron Commander informed me that he thought I had accomplished my mission and I needed to prepare for my next assignment. His decision was based solely on the fact that I had been in the combat zone for 30 out of 32 months. I reluctantly agreed to return to Fort Irwin as part of the advance party to help facilitate the return of the squadron. I arrived in December at Fort Irwin, and within 10 days I was off to Fort Benning.

The battle rhythm and structure at Fort Benning seemed to be just what the doctor had ordered: a place where every day I felt I was contributing to the war effort without getting into a vehicle and leaving the Forward Operating Base to establish a check point, visit an outpost, or go to a memorial service. I felt that I was part of something that really mattered. As I grew into the position, it became easier. I was surrounded by remarkable leadership such as then Colonel Charles Durr and another passionate leader, Colonel Bill Simril, who had a Soldier's heart, for sure. With them, it was always about the Soldiers and their families, not about themselves. In a couple months, tragedy hit again. A first sergeant from a sister brigade lost his life in a motorcycle accident, and I called the Brigade CSM, reaching out to him and understanding all too well what the loss of life meant to the unit.

The Brigade Commander and I went to the memorial service; it was then that the flashbacks from combat began to challenge me. This memorial service and the ones I had attended in Iraq seemed to fuse together. I was here and there at the same moment in time. I tried to separate myself from everyone else. With the playing of Taps, my heart felt as if it would stop at any second. My hands shook, so I grabbed onto the bench in front of us. Then I found myself unable to look up as the tears rolled down my face.

I thought to myself," I am in trouble. Get a grip, take a deep breath and relax."

As I would learn later, I was entering the early phases of building resilience. I was attempting to bounce back and separate the current situation from the past ones. Separating *then* from *now* sounds simple. But with PTS, it becomes a question of survival, and you *must* separate your past from the here and now. The past was at every corner, on bill boards, everywhere . . .

CHAPTER 11

The Sound of Guns Firing

A few months went by, the challenges continued, and I avoided the firing ranges. I would even contact a unit to get their arrival and departure times so I could avoid the actual exercise. I would find a way not to be there when actual rounds were fired. The sound of weapons firing brought back the bad memories of combat. A Command Sergeant Major's inability to cope with the sounds of rifles seems strange, but somehow I rationalized it. In the spring of 2006, I was supposed to head to Fort Jackson to attend the Pre-Command Course for leaders, but that too became a challenge. One Friday, I walked out of the Headquarters building to go running. But I couldn't. Sharp pains in my stomach and groin area kept me from running at all. I went to the Troop Medical Clinic. I then went to the hospital. The pain was unbearable. The doctor did test after test and determined that I had some internal stomach issues that would take time to heal. I received a ten-day "no running" profile and headed to Fort Jackson to attend the Army's Pre-Command Course for Command Sergeant Majors and Unit Commanders at brigade and battalion levels.

I arrived at Fort Jackson on Sunday afternoon, and while I was watching TV, an announcement came over the news about new attacks in Baghdad. I listened carefully, taking in every second of the broadcast. Later that night, my spouse found me sitting up in bed crying, challenged by the thoughts of a nightmare. I was almost inconsolable.

I was mumbling, "Why not me? Why did they have to die instead of me?"

This behavior began occurring nightly. I would fall asleep and wake up in a cold sweat, sobbing and screaming from nightmares. I started working out two and sometimes three times a day to be as tired as possible before I went to sleep. "A few beers at night, just to relax," I thought would help. Soon it became a lot of beer.

CHAPTER 12

The Death of a Best Friend's Son

At this point, I would like to take a few moments to share some thoughts on the patriotism of our great country as it relates to Ringgold, GA, and a town I was saddened to visit this last weekend in Kentucky.

The Soldier's creed says, "I am a warrior and a member of a team. I will never leave a fallen comrade."

That was never shown more truly than it was at a funeral I attended on Saturday, September 30, 2006, in London, Kentucky, for SFC Jason Jones.

On Thursday, September 21, I received a call that a good friend of mine had passed away. With many messages, the first report is almost always wrong. I was emotionally drained by the time I realized that this information was inadequate. Unfortunately, the real message was worse than I could have imagined.

Colonel Charlie Jones, a friend and fellow warrior, had deployed to Iraq last spring, along with his 29-year-old son, Jason. The message was informing me of the death of Colonel Jones's son, who had died on September 21, while defending our country in Iraq. Unfortunately, the message was incomplete and just said that a good friend had died in Iraq.

Colonel Charlie Jones is one of the best Soldiers I have ever served with in my 29-year career in the United States Army. I contacted him after he returned from Iraq on September 23. To say the least, I was tongue-tied in starting a conversation about the death of his son.

After a few minutes, a great conversation evolved, during which I grew up about 10 years from listening to the Colonel's words. He acknowledged the great American Soldier that his son had been during his Army career with his willingness to put his life into harm's way for our country. It was, to say the least, a blessing for me to hear that from him, first hand. This man had just made the ultimate sacrifice of his own son to the cause of freedom.

Too many of our fellow Americans have chosen not to support the war effort that our country has undertaken. I challenge them to take a moment and recognize the huge sacrifice that all our service members make daily on their behalf.

On September 30, I traveled from Fort Benning, GA, to London, KY, the longest journey I had taken in a while. This journey was in some ways tougher than my trips to Iraq on three separate occasions. It's tough enough to drive these days and remain focused on the roads and the other drivers, but this day was tougher. I had not seen my friend since my deployment to Iraq in 2003. We had been in constant contact by email over the last three years, and he had called my wife on several occasions to ensure she was doing well while I was deployed.

This death brought back the memories of the numerous memorials that I had attended in Iraq for my Soldiers as well as for fellow Soldiers of other units. These memories are the worst part of fighting for our country. You try to shake them by staying busy and occupied. Then another great American Soldier dies in Iraq or Afghanistan and the thoughts come back full circle. Any day that I am driving down some road here at Benning when loud explosions and gunfire ring out, I have to take a deep breath, as it is all too similar to real war. I know all too well that every Soldier's death affects my heart, and all Soldiers fighting for our country mean more to me than anything.

I arrived about 90 minutes early, took a moment to remember Jason, and walked outside. I was excited to see approximately 500 bikers with American Flags. Who were these people? They were the Patriot Guard Riders from Kentucky and the surrounding region.

They had mobilized to defend our American hero's honor and to prevent those who wanted to protest from dishonoring him. I sat in amazement and said I needed to thank every one of these folks. As I reached out my hand to the first man, my eyes watered. I could barely contain my inner thought of how proud I was to be among these Patriot saints. I started at the front and walked my way through the crowd of bikers.

I am sure that all of our fallen comrades looked down that day. As we were completing the funeral services at the cemetery, a slight rain began to fall. Perhaps the angels were crying with happy tears.

I could not imagine what our society of Americans thought until this funeral. I had become discouraged by recent media talk. However, I was convinced of American patriotism by these observations:

- The number of people who attended the funeral and the number of people who just came and stood outside the funeral home, showing the American flag in support of this fallen Soldier.
- A Gold Star mother, with a daughter of a deceased Soldier, paying homage to Charlie's son. What a painful memory that must have been to her, yet you could see she was so proud of her kid. She was there to support the Joneses.
- The professionalism of the local and state police who provided security and controlled traffic, and the respect they paid to a fallen Soldier as the procession wound its way to the cemetery.
- The citizens of Kentucky who pulled over onto the side on the road as the funeral procession went past. They could have kept driving, but they chose not to.
- The number of people stopping their lawn work to pay respect to the funeral procession that passed by.
- The Kentucky governor who sat in a pew very inconspicuously, but he was there to support the family.
- The bikers and other supporters who, by their sheer numbers, blocked out the view of the protestors. You knew the protestors showed up only because our beloved media thought it was important you know about this frivolous protest.

- The professionalism of the Kentucky National Guard Soldiers and their leaders in taking care of the family, the conduct of the 21-gun salute, taps, and the helicopter flyover.
- A mother out on the front porch in Keavy, Kentucky, saluting every damn car as it passed by with American flags waving. I wondered why she did this. Seemed to me she either had a son over there or knew what it means to sacrifice, or maybe she is just a great American.
- A young boy with a crew cut, about 9 or 10 years old, holding a hand over his heart as the procession neared the cemetery.

Some of these thoughts are from a fellow warrior who served with me. Yes, I borrowed them to explain some of my feelings and ensure I captured the essence of patriotism. London, KY, reminded me of Ringgold, GA. When I had come back to Ringgold three years before, we saw the flags of all our great service members who are no longer with us. One of these flags is for my father, who had served our country proudly. These flags stand in honor of these great Soldiers. I am happy to say there is at least one other city with this attitude in America, and I am sure that there are many more. I am satisfied now that patriotism is alive and well, despite the critics.

When the funeral ended, I had several hours to reflect with my friend. As we talked, I told Charlie about my anger that the protestors had come.

Charlie replied, "Sam, It just tells me that what we are doing is right."

I paused with amazement. Then I said, "Charlie, I wish just one of them would confront me directly."

He replied, "That's a horse of a different color." I knew exactly what that meant.

After that comment, I knew that this great Soldier was doing well. Despite the loss of his only son and his own soon return to combat, his pain was easing. I knew his heart would be always with Jason, but his mind was with his troops in Iraq. He was excited about returning to complete his mission and bring the remainder of his troops home safely.

Please continue to support our troops and pray for them often. It's these American heroes who are giving us the opportunity to sleep through the night without worry.

A NOTE TO THE READER FROM COLONEL JONES:

I first met Command Sergeant Major (Retired) Samuel M. Rhodes upon reporting to duty as the Brigade Executive Officer of a Training Support Brigade in January, 2001. Assignment to a multi-component unit is a unique experience for anyone, even more so when you are one of two National Guard officers assigned to an active component unit. When the Brigade Command Sergeant Major was introducing me to the staff, I met an energetic young operations sergeant by the name of Sam Rhodes, aka Rocky. I'm no military intelligence officer, but it didn't take long to figure out why the Command affectionately referred to Command Sergeant Major Rhodes as Rocky! As a person and Soldier, Sam has an innate sense of loyalty, duty, respect, selfless service, honor, integrity and personal courage. Those qualities, coupled with his ability to bring out the best of others by his example, make him "Solid as a Rock"—thus the name, Rocky. I quickly attached myself to Master Sergeant Rhodes to ensure I was up to speed and running in the most effective and efficient manner possible. Our teacher, coach, and mentor relationship developed into a strong friendship that has endured for more than 12 years. The chapter you have just read is a reflection of our friendship, our brotherhood and our bond. In September, 2006, my friend stood shoulder to shoulder with me and my family during my son's funeral.

With our veterans committing suicide at an epidemic rate of 22 suicides per day, the chains of stigma must be broken. This book is a reflection of Sam Rhodes's personal experiences; he wears the proverbial tee-shirt. One doesn't experience life without experiencing life-changing events. It's how one handles those changes that counts. This book addresses ways to handle those changes to effect a positive outcome. Some have said that nothing can prevent persons who are intent on killing themselves from doing so. Mental health treatment is not the new silver bullet, and psychotherapists are not magicians. The epidemic of military and veteran suicides requires action on multiple levels. But our strongest ally in this fight is hidden in plain sight—the most powerful motivator for service members and veterans—their love for, and the love of, their buddies. Look no further than CSM Samuel M. Rhodes to foster what that looks like. He understands that we need to mobilize that ally immediately. Some will still argue that we cannot stop someone intent on taking his/ her own life. CSM Rhodes takes offense with that assertion, as all leaders must. CSM Rhodes asserts that to break the chain of stigma is to effectively remove the elephant in the room.

Through his powerful influence on my personal life and wellbeing, I know firsthand that CSM Rhodes is committed to removing all barriers to changing and improving the lives of our Soldiers and veterans. By extending your hand to a fellow brother or sister veteran who is struggling with Post Traumatic Stress Disorder, you can bring about that change. By breaking down barriers one by one, you will be "breaking the chains of stigma."

Charles T. Jones
COL, KYARNG
Deputy Chief of Staff Personnel

other. Yes, I became fluent in bad Spanish expressions. I still recall some of those words to this day.

Near the end of basic training, with one more day of training to do at the MOUT site, the drill sergeant screamed, "Get down the damn rope, Rhodes."

For some reason I did just that; unfortunately it was the wrong way. I released my hands and fell to the ground, not realizing what had happened and the adrenalin was flowing. I jumped up and ran over to my rucksack. Within several minutes, we were on the road headed back. As we began walking, I remember being tired, and my ankles and feet were hurting more than usual for that period of training. I don't recall much after that except that I woke up in Martin Army Community Hospital with two broken ankles. I was hurting, but more worried about being recycled and not graduating. I had already been there more than enough for my liking. Drill Sergeant Wall, who was very good at his job, came to visit me. He asked how I was doing. I explained that l just wanted to get back to training.

He said, "Take your time and get better. I will take care of you."

The next day I had crutches and was off to my unit. They put me on quarters so I was still missing training. I envisioned going back to another company, and I was not happy, to say the least, about that option. Fortunately for me, I was an 11H Anti-Armor Crewman, and the training was for 11B Infantrymen, so I didn't miss anything. All of the Military Occupational Specialty had split the training requirements. As an 11H, I was not required to endure a lot of physical training. However, being extremely motivated to succeed, I pushed myself all the time to finish ahead of the pack at everything. Therefore, as several weeks passed, I continued to do as many pushups and exercises as I could. Time doesn't slow down for injuries; the final Army Physical Fitness Test (APFT) came before I could get healed. Drill Sergeant Walls told me that I couldn't take the Army Physical Fitness Test. I insisted that I was sure I could pass it.

Drill Sergeant Walls finally said, "Okay, I will let you take it, but don't hurt yourself."

The next day I woke up, tightened up my ankle supports, and got fired up. I breezed through the events, and then came the final challenge—the two-mile run in boots.

Drill Sergeant Walls came up to me and commented, "Rhodes, you amaze me. Just go out there and do your best. Don't hurt yourself."

At the end of the first lap I found myself in the top 10, running as fast as I could. Drill Sergeant Walls was smiling and loudly cheering for me. By the time I finished, I had the third fastest time of the day. Walls was extremely proud of me and my efforts, so much so that he used me as an example for other platoons.

"You see Rhodes? Even my broken private can run faster than you 'Joes.'" (a term of endearment to us privates).

My career took shape from that point, and before I realized it, I was headed to Fort Campbell, KY. Within nine months, I became the Battalion and Brigade Soldier of the Quarter and runner-up for the Fort Campbell Installation Soldier of the Year for 1981. Fort Campbell would provide certain things that I wouldn't forget.

I had arrived at Fort Campbell in mid-summer. As I recall, most of the Soldiers I met had been in the Army for six to eight years, and they were heavy drinkers and smokers. I thought the fellow who did the driving was a crazy man. He was Specialist Barnes, who always joked with us, "Hang on back there or I will throw your ass off."

Yes, and that's what he did, too! Several days into our training we got a change in mission, as I understand it now. We were to move, secure an area, and provide over watch. Barnes, who had one speed, hit every bump he could; he excelled at that. After about an hour, he caught me off guard and threw my ass out of the vehicle. I landed on top of a five-gallon fuel canister guard which cut a six-inch gap in my leg that required a medical evacuation. I remember 1st Lt Robinson, the CO, asking me what had happened.

I replied, "Sir, I fell."

Specialist Barnes had already given me the nine lines, warning me not to mention how I got hurt. He was about 6'5, 220 pounds, and of course I agreed to obey the Specialist.

That tour in Fort Campbell went by so quickly, that I barely remember getting married and welcoming my first child, Amanda, into this world.

In May of 1982, I was sent to Friedberg, Germany. Having never been far from home, I was enchanted when I arrived at my barracks. There were 20-foot ceilings and no Soldiers were there. They had been alerted that morning to go to the border. It turned out to be the toughest tour that I can remember. Being away from home and the daughter that I loved as much as I loved Amanda made it tougher. Did I mention I was a 21-year-old in a foreign country alone, without even fellow soldiers?

I remember calling home and saying, "I am going AWOL. I hate it here."

All those thoughts really consumed me. When the Soldiers returned, I, a corporal now, was tossed into the mix—Charge of Quarters, NCO of the Quarter, Section Leader. It all happened so quickly.

In September of 1982, my former spouse, Carol, was sick, so I returned home to Talladega, Alabama, for emergency leave. Little did I realize what that leave would cost me.

It took several weeks for my wife to get better, and then I was off to Friedberg, Germany, again. When I arrived, the platoon sergeant called me in.

"Corporal Rhodes, how is your family doing?"

"Fine, now. My daughter is growing fast."

"That's good, because for the rest of your 18 months you aren't going anywhere."

I didn't, either. In July of 1983, my son, Sam Rhodes Jr., was born. I had to settle for getting pictures. Seven months later, I learned that he was already walking!

It was May 22, 1984, when reality hit me hard. I had started the out processing to head home. First Sergeant called for me, and I thought, "Oh no, what now?" First Sergeant Brown was all business, as I remembered. When I graduated from a Primary Leader Development course, I came back from school wanting to make a difference, wanting to be a leader. First Sergeant thought differently. I learned that day that leading is an instinct, not a skill to be learned. When we learn to appreciate our Soldiers and understand them, we become leaders. Leadership is not acquired by simply telling Soldiers how many mistakes they make. I moved out quickly to the orderly room. After all these months, I was not looking forward to any more ass-chewing, for sure. As I entered the room, I could sense a quiet calm in the air.

First Sergeant met me, shook my hand, and said, "Have a seat, SGT Rhodes."

My best friend, SGT Ken Howard, was there, and I was becoming anxious.

"I am sorry to tell you this, SGT Rhodes. Your father passed away on May 19."

In some strange way, I was relieved and saddened at the same time. As my eyes began to water, Ken Howard stood up, I stood up, and he embraced me as he never had before.

Ken said, "I love you, Rho Rho," using the name his young son always called me. He knew just how much I longed to see my own son.

I was shocked, but I understood what my father had been through in World War II and what health problems he now had. He had suffered five heart attacks before I even graduated from school. He still had shrapnel in his leg from the war. I was so grateful to learn that my mom had refused to bury my dad until I returned home. I returned home for his memorial service and his burial. The Veterans of Foreign Wars honored him with the graveside honors we now provide every Soldier and veteran.

It was a fast turnaround, as I then headed to Fort Lewis and back to Germany for three and a half years. Time had gone by so fast. Before I realized it, I had gone from a private at Ft. Benning to a drill sergeant in charge of the privates. I spent the better part of 1989-1992 training infantry men to participate in Desert Storm. I remember just how rewarding it was. Our commander, Lt. COL Mark Gerner, was a committed leader, and having battled cancer, he certainly understood what life's challenges were all about.

I remember the graduation day of a platoon of COHART Soldiers that were headed to Fort Campbell, Kentucky. This was a special platoon; we had won all the awards, Best BRM, High APFT, Best Marching Platoon and even Honor Platoon. All of that meant nothing to me; I had done that before. The one difference was the Soldiers' respect.

I was asked that day, "Drill Sergeant, are you staying late today?"

I asked why it mattered. They didn't answer, but later, after graduation, I found three Soldiers and my spouse on my front lawn.

I immediately yelled at them, "What are you doing here?"

Private Craig spoke up. "Drill Sergeant, you told us all you needed was a bucket of fried chicken."

I laughed. They stayed for a few minutes and then left. I was like a proud dad. It got even better. A few days later, about 3 AM, the phone rang and my spouse handed it to me. Being out of cycle, I was surprised.

It was Pvt. Craig who said, "Drill Sergeant, we're leaving tomorrow."

I paused. "Craig, are you packed up?"

"Yes. The entire platoon is going. Are you okay? I just wanted to thank you for all you did for us. I believe I am as trained as I ever could have been."

Wow! I was speechless for a moment, and then I asked,

"Remember the times we covered our eyes and were able to put the M16 together, blindfolded?"

He said that he remembered.

"I want you to imagine now that same scenario. You're going to war, blindfolded. What did you do when you couldn't see your weapon parts?"

Private Craig replied, "I put it together with the instincts you instilled in me from practicing over and over again."

I told him, "Basic training and advance infantry training have provided you with the instinct to fight and win on today's battlefield. All of the training and the repeated training have provided you a foundation. Utilize that and call me when you get home."

I never heard from Craig again and wondered how he was doing. Several years later, I ran into him. He was a young staff sergeant doing well in our Army.

I left Fort Benning and headed to Fort Lewis, Washington, to be a platoon sergeant. Within a matter of months, I was the First Sergeant as an SFC. I was reassigned to be the Advance Party BRAC NCOIC for the 2nd Armor Cavalry Regiments and moved from Fort Lewis to Fort Polk. I welcomed that opportunity because my family had remained in Alabama. Months went by really fast as the regiment arrived and transitioned to an Armored Cavalry Regiment. Soon I found myself on orders to Fort Stewart, Ga. I called the Department of the Army to ask why I was moving again.

The Department of the Army representative in my branch said, "You're an 11H Heavy Anti-Armor Weapon Crewman. You're not authorized to be at Fort Polk."

I thought about it and said, "Okay, that makes sense."

A tragic turn of events occurred that led me to a 90-day compassionate reassignment to Fort McCallen, Alabama. I pushed through it and returned to Fort Stewart, GA, to assume my duties as the platoon sergeant of an Anti-Tank Platoon. When we found out that our battalion was deploying, we all got excited. Having missed Desert Storm, I thought this was my opportunity to do my part. About three days before we were to leave, the Company Commander had a meeting. He announced that we were attached to another battalion now, and we were going to begin turning in all our M901 Improved TOW vehicles. Surprised, I asked a dumb question.

"What does that mean?"

The Company Commander replied, "The Army has decided to deactivate our company and reassign everyone."

Common sense was running thin at this point. About two weeks later, after the battalion departed without us, I found out that I was going to become a 19 series. I was angry. If the Army had made this move four months ago, I could have stayed at Fort Polk.

As life would have it, the change was a welcome one. I learned so much during the transition from Infantry Platoon Sergeant to Armor Platoon Sergeant, it was amazing. The jobs were the same for the most part. The tactics were similar, but I now had a more lethal piece of equipment. I spent four months in 1995 in Basic and Advanced Armor Training with about 160 young Soldiers. To be honest, I spent most of my time in amazement at what we had to do to make Armor Crewmen. Later in May, 1996, I was assigned to 1-64 Armor as an Operations Sergeant, and I deployed to Intrinsic Action. I became a Platoon Sergeant for an Armor Platoon and then was reassigned in 1997 to be a First Sergeant. My Army career was a wonderful experience. I met and learned so much from so many people, I cannot begin to fathom all the information I have acquired.

The toughest decision I would ever make came in 2002. The Army had selected me to be a Sergeant Major and to attend the United States Army Sergeant Majors Academy as part of Class 53. Having been a committed Soldier for many years, I realized that in the coming months, something was going to occur. I wanted to be a part of it this time, because my assignments had diverted me from harm's way on many previous occasions. I informed the Department of the Army that my preference was to go to a unit that would deploy, instead of to the

Academy. Mrs. Parson, from DA, informed me that she would enroll me in Distance Learning Class 26 and that I could be reassigned. That wish came sooner than I expected. In November, 2002, I was promoted to Sergeant Major, and I reported to Fort Polk, LA. Upon arrival I was assigned to 3rd Squadron, 2nd Armored Cavalry Regiment. In April, 2003, we got the call. I boarded a plane and headed to Kuwait as part of the advance party for the 2nd ACR Regimental Headquarters. I was selected to be the Regimental Operations SGM. The next 32 months would prove to be the toughest of my life!

Having been to Kuwait before, I knew way too well the surroundings, so it was simple to adjust. My first priority was ensuring that I had a place for all our Soldiers to rest and prepare to cross the Line of Departure into Iraq. I was, of course, anxious. I remembered all too well those stories from my father and the former Governor about the loss of their friends and the impact that it had made upon them. Thinking that it was a good possibility that I would become a casualty, based on the estimated loss of life from the initial surge into Iraq, I wrote more and more as each day passed.

After the main body arrived, as we were preparing to unload the ship that had brought all our vehicles and equipment, we received a call. The call was from a Soldier whom we had left at the camp.

"Sir, the tents are on fire. We're trying to put the fire out, but the ammunition is going off!"

Yes, we had made some dumb decisions. We had placed small arms ammunition into living areas with weapons. By the time we returned, about six tents had been destroyed and 250 soldiers had lost all or part of their gear. These Soldiers included the Command Group, the Squadron Commander, the Command Sergeant Major, and me—critical staff folks.

Having built a repetition for getting the job done with little guidance, I immediately visited the local Army's Exchange that was in the camp. I talked to the manager and told him what had occurred. My goal was to make each Soldier comfortable with a blanket, pillow, and personal hygiene items for the night. I did just that.

The next morning I received a call to come to the Regimental Tactical Operations Center.

I was greeted with this question, "SGM, did you authorize the purchase of over $20,000 of gear for Soldiers?"

Shocked at being asked this question, I replied, "Roger that, Sir."

After a few words were exchanged, I returned to the mission at hand, believing that a smart person would figure it all out. Never was it mentioned to me again.

When we crossed the border headed to Iraq, I was part of the advance party again. How sweet is that? At least there wouldn't be any surprises. We already knew that some poor hungry locals would try to take our gear as we crossed. We had tied everything down and rehearsed how to use sticks instead of bullets to warn them off.

Once I was in Iraq, I became accustomed to the setting rather easily. I was amazed by the children and saddened by the way they had to live. As we got closer to Baghdad, I could see that the "rich get richer" idea was well ingrained there.

On May 23, 2003, I had a life-altering encounter. There was a sudden attack on our base camp, and as the power went out, someone screamed that the roof-top guard had been injured. A fellow Soldier and I rushed to the roof. Everyone was worried about second and third attacks, so it took a moment to access the area before we could get to the wounded Soldier. He was shot through one side and out the other. We stabilized him and carried him down.

This was just the beginning for me; I was traumatized, not knowing what to think, and instinctively, I started barking out orders and giving directions to secure the camp. We had arrived just a few days earlier and we were still in the early stages of doing a complete assessment to ensure that security was tight.

Now looking back, I realize that this was one of the many critical decisions that I would be making. I didn't realize then the importance of those decisions. Having just had my first encounter with seeing a fellow warrior bleeding, providing him some help, and then worrying about him, I found myself becoming anxious and scared. I had to make a decision to not be scared, not be afraid, and absolutely not show any weakness whatsoever. I had to toughen up and accomplish the mission. I needed to be a strong leader and conceal the remorse or the pain I was feeling for the wounded Soldier. I told all the Soldiers as we reinforced the surroundings that they had to remain situational aware all the time.

Who is our enemy? Everyone is. I repeated that same idea over and over again until I felt they understood it. Over the next 15 months of OIF 1 & 2 we encountered the enemy at every angle. There were mortar attacks, rocket attacks, small arms fire and IED's. In July, 2003, after being made the Regimental Operations SGM, I wrote several letters to the families of the 23 Soldiers with me.

I decided that some of my Soldiers were far too experienced to be in this group and needed to be down at the squadron level. That decision almost cost a Soldier his life. I told SPC Green to pack his bags and move to the squadron level. Yes, I told him why. I mentioned career enhancement, seniority—all the standard stuff. Two days later, while on patrol, his vehicle was hit with an IED. He was not seriously wounded, but I left the Forward Operation Base immediately to go to the Combat Support Hospital. When I arrived I found him in good spirits. As I looked at him and held his hand, I thought, "Did I cause this?"

He looked as if he knew what I was thinking. He said, "SGM, it's not your fault. I volunteered for this patrol."

I left the room and chose to walk around and talk to numerous Soldiers. One Soldier worried about his buddy; another Soldier was just happy to be alive. That was the norm throughout the hospital. I felt that I was extremely blessed. The sights and sounds of this hospital left me challenged at night. I was unable to sleep. When I did sleep, I would sleepwalk and wake up wondering how I got to where I was. One day we heard explosions, so we climbed to the roof of our sleeping quarters to see how far away they were. They were several miles away, but so huge that we thought they were right outside the FOB. That night was a turning point for me. I didn't realize that the malaria pills I was taking could cause side effects, one of which could be a mood-altering disorder that could lead to sleepwalking. I relived the day's events and sleepwalked to the top of the building. I awoke, to my displeasure, on the top of that building; I was scared and I wondered how I had gotten there.

The next morning I went to see a physician assistant and told him what had occurred. His diagnosis was that the medicine probably had caused the sleepwalking, and he recommended that I stop taking it. However, this had not been my first encounter with sleepwalking. I immediately began tying my leg to the bunk that I slept on. I also put stuff up against the door to keep me from exiting during those nights in which I didn't tie myself up.

The attack that followed would continue to haunt me later in my career. I remember all too well the attack on the United Nations building and the XO for the regiment calling me and saying the Regimental Commander wanted me there immediately. I arrived to one of the worst scenes of death and destruction that I had ever seen in my life. The United Nations Ambassador was still alive under the rubble. Later we found out that he had made a call to get help, but then he died. The people in the immediate blast were covered with glass, and many of them were dead. We secured the area and established a perimeter.

About two days later, my driver and I were headed to the UN area, and just up ahead, a matter of eight seconds away, a vehicle exploded, killing several Iraqi police.

I never imagined how close death and destruction would come to me until that year in the Middle East. As a leader, I remained calm, cool, and collected in public. There were many days spent with the chaplain and friends discussing how terrible some of these terrorist attacks had become. I had always appreciated life and the simple ways that it could pass you by. Certainly this wasn't any different from losing a friend or family back home. However, each day we were in this country, we observed death.

One day my Soldiers and I were driving down Canal Street when we came upon two bodies in the middle of the road. They had been killed the night before. We didn't realize why, or what message was being sent by putting them in the middle of the street. We just remained quiet; each Soldier in my patrol had his own thoughts. I could see it in their faces. I realized, as death came closer, how precious life really is. In some ways, I began to realize how I was changing a little each day. I began not calling home as much; I had less desire to write. The exception was that I made efforts on numerous occasions to write to the families of my Soldiers to let them know how their guys were doing.

When I receive an e-mail from someone's family, it usually begins with "Sir," not "Sergeant Major." You know, we enlisted folks sometimes joke about how we are not sirs; we work for a living. Having spent most of my 29 years in the military as a leader at some level, I have grown to love officers. They truly demonstrate their desire to prepare Soldiers, both in combat and at home, for what's next. Sometimes, an enlisted man thinks about how to get things done quickly without always considering what might happen later. An officer, from my experience through the development process, always has a better understanding of where the situation goes next. He has a vision, of sorts. Yes, enlisted Soldiers use their hands to work for a living. Officers work just as hard with their minds. It's a team effort; one can't move forward without the other.

A short while after my first letter to a family, I received an email from a mom. It simply thanked me for the letter. Her son was an SPC and hadn't written or called for several months. When I got this message, I notified the Platoon Sergeant to have this Soldier visit me in the Regimental Tactical Operation Center. When he arrived there a short while later, I started the conversation by asking him to tell me about himself and his Army service. I always like using signs and gestures to communicate or to stop communication. As we continued to speak about the Army, I placed my Index finger over my lips to indicate, "Okay, I got it." I asked him if he were married, and he said that he wasn't and that he lived with his mother and father. I jokingly said, "I have two beautiful daughters," and showed him their picture. I had him confused. A Sergeant Major doesn't spend a lot of time talking about family. He was wondering where I was going. Then I asked how his mom was. I could see the amazement on his face. We talked a little about my own father and mother and how I had failed miserably over my career to stay in contact with them. I admitted forgetting what an impact they had had on my life. I didn't tell the Soldier to write to his family, but about two weeks later I got a thank you note from his mom. She said, "I don't know what you said to my son, but I have received three letters this week."

That note gave me the desire to keep writing. I wrote hundreds of letters after that, not only to parents, but to my hometown newspaper, keeping everyone informed about the Iraq War.

Along with writing letters, I had to remain focused and situation aware at all times. I developed a sixth sense to second guess what we were doing and provide my advice and recommendations to the leaders above me to help us through the combat tour that would be extended soon to July, 2004. I remember that day so clearly, as if it happened yesterday. I was sitting in the Tactical Operations Center on April 4, 2004, the day we were supposed to be relieved by First Cavalry. An hour before the change, a unit had come under fire in Sadr City in Baghdad. The initial message said that they had received small arms fire, but before we realized it, there were multiple engagements. The enemy had surprised us that day. I can't say a lot about this. When it was over, we had lost eight Soldiers and suffered over 55 wounded ones in just a few hours.

It was one of the largest dust offs that had occurred since the Iraq War had begun. I began to think that we were not going anywhere. We were going to stay longer. All my Soldiers had been excited about going home. We even had Soldiers already on the way home. I still remained calm, with no desire to go home. I just wanted to remain in contact. For me, this had become my home for the time being. As we travel throughout our careers in the Army, we adjust to our location and know that within a couple years we will be going to another place. This time I didn't feel that way. I felt as if we had to stay here where we were needed. We had so much to do.

I received the word from the Operations Officer that I was to move my Soldiers and establish the Tactical Operations Center and another Forward Operation Base, in preparation for staging the regiment's move to the Najaf Area of Iraq. I became instantly motivated, knowing we were staying. I was excited; others simply became overwhelmed in the moment. I began barking out orders and letting Soldiers know what to do and where we were going.

The first night at the temporary FOB we received a warm welcome from our closest friend—a mortar barrage. A Soldier ran into my sleep area, reporting that we were under attack. I told him to go back to sleep, keep his helmet and sap vest on, and not worry.

Deep inside me, I wondered if they had secured this FOB. I knew a patrol would automatically be heading toward the site from which the firing had come. We would counterattack, but running from a firing location was a simple process for the enemy. More often than not, we wouldn't get any battle damage from counter fire.

Three days later, I got some more good news. I was asked to lead the first patrol south. Whoa! I was told to take 40 vehicles with me as part of the Division Tactical Operations Center! I wondered whose stupid idea that was! Minutes later I found out that SGM of the DCG Tactical Operations Center and his security would be in my convoy. I was stunned. Not only did I have to worry about my Soldiers, now I also had someone else to worry about. I briefed the entire patrol, ensuring that everyone knew the route and knew the actions on contact. There was always guess work, such as what would happen if we got hit at the front of the convoy. Okay, I realized that I was to be in the second vehicle in the patrol. Knowing that I would be in the vehicle most likely to be hit, I needed to react well to that situation and remain in control of the convoy. What about the middle or the back? Throughout the convoy, I placed key folks that I knew could handle the pressure of attacks.

We took off on the convoy and everything went smoothly for the first 20 or so kilometers. We took a short halt to rest and regain some focus. About 15 minutes later we moved out again. Approximately five minutes later, I heard a pop. Instantly, the gunner from the lead vehicle opened fire. The gunner, SPC Harris, was the man in my book that day; he probably single-handedly saved the convoy. When I heard the pop and the machine gun fire opening up, I turned to watch as the RPG went over my vehicle. Simultaneously, I watched SPC Harris remove the enemy as an obstacle. Out of the corner of my eye, I saw another RPG coming to my front. This time it seemed certain it was going to hit us, but for some reason it went over my truck and hit the truck behind me. The vehicle was damaged and the driver was hurt, but like many RPG's, this one didn't explode. I then observed a truck with 10 or 12 armed insurgents approaching us from the west at a fast pace. Immediately I opened fire with my M4, and SPC Harris and several others began firing as well. That was a good day for the home team. When it was all said and done, we estimated that we had killed at least 12 insurgents that day and survived at least five RPG's that were fired into our convoy, mostly at the front vehicles. We continued up the road and did another short halt. The call from the rear told us that all had cleared the engagement area and all was good. We continued to the camp in the south.

I have struggled for the last few years to understand the importance of that particular attack on our convoy. It was also an attack on my own mental stability. I find myself feeling the loss of not only our own great service members, but also of those we have killed. Like us, they think they are defending their country and their families. These feelings represent another experience that we as Soldiers have and most people can only fantasize about. Taking another's life has consequences! A friend of mine and I talk all the time about this. The mind continues to churn with deep thoughts as the anniversary of each battle occurs. It's not a memory that we can erase.

The next day I got a call to come to the TAC. The DCG from 1st Armored Division had arrived, and he had received the report. His team had credited me and my security team for getting them here safely. He thanked me and told me to let him know if I needed anything. I acknowledged his comments and continued my duties. It had been a close call.

As we continued our three month extension, I became more and more engaged with the enemy, attempting to win hearts and minds. I worked to do humanitarian aide projects to help the locals. My team visited areas that appeared as if they had been abandoned for a long while. When we talked to the local school master, he showed us what he needed to educate the children in the region, as well as to improve the conditions in the schools. Those conditions were horrible. The summers were very hot in Iraq. The classrooms had no windows and no air conditioning. I assured the head master that we would help. I talked to the unit and before we knew it, we started receiving school supplies and even CERP funds to help rebuild this school. The head master was excited. Through my interpreter, he thanked me for what 2nd ACR was doing. He said that it all helped but that he still needed this, that and the other thing. He asked me to meet with the community leaders for a discussion, and I agreed to schedule a day to meet.

The next day a patrol, coming by the school on the way to FOB Duke where we had established a new home, was hit by an IED right across the road from the school. When I received the report, I immediately became angry and called for my patrol security team. We headed for the school and found only the head master there. Through the interpreter, I asked him who had done this. The head master was very reluctant to say anything. He finally got the message that unless he helped me, I was not going to help him anymore. There would be no water line, no second school up the road, and no more food every two days or so. He finally told us that some strangers from another area had taken up a site about two clicks off the road. We searched and searched the area, but with no luck. I informed the head master of the school that if there was one more attack, we would stop everything. The remaining three months were quiet in that area.

This tour took its toll on the regiment; twenty-one regimental troopers lost their lives in Iraq. The death of these warriors weighed heavily on my heart as time moved me closer and closer to coming back to the States. Yes, I had stopped thinking about home many months before, only seeing it as a departure from where my fellow Soldiers gave their all. There was one Soldier in particular, whom I had met while in Iraq, who was a friend of the Regimental CSM. We would get together on occasion with other sergeant majors and talk about the good times. On one such occasion, back in December, 2003, we did just that, and little did I realize that one of us would soon be taken.

I was resting in my room on the day before Christmas, when someone knocked on my door. The knock became loud, and the voice of the Regimental CSM called out that Eric Cook had just been killed by an IED. My heart seemed to stop for a moment. I couldn't imagine that it was true. A brigade level CSM, who loved his Soldiers, had been taken from us. I got up immediately and went to the TOC; I listened as the radio reports came through. There was nothing about Eric. The long night dragged on. The next day, Christmas, 2003, I just stayed to myself, trying to clear my mind. The chaplain came by to talk, but I really wasn't in the mood for listening. I just couldn't understand.

The pain from the loss of every Soldier whose memorial I attended was special; I tried to celebrate his life and put a positive spin on it when talking to other Soldiers. However, when I was alone I would find myself becoming more and more emotional. Some people say it's okay to cry. I hope so, because I needed to do just that many times.

. As the tour came to an end, I knew that I wanted to stay. Many regimental Soldiers felt the same way, but we are Soldiers and we go where we are told. That is what we do. However, the one advantage to being a sergeant major is that you sometimes get a vote. I contacted the SGM branch and worked my way back to Georgia. During the process, I was selected for Command Sergeant Major and would have to wait to get a battalion. I worked my way on the staff of one of the finest officers in this man's Army, Lieutenant General Steven Whitcomb, who was then the Commander of 3rd United States Army.

After deploying again in January, 2005, I lost too many Soldiers, and many others had sustained wounds. At one point in early April, I thought we had started into a new phase of our ongoing operation. It was just then when the deaths of my Soldiers quickly went from zero to six in just twenty-four days, with almost two dozen wounded. The enemy had to get a vote and they did. We mourned the loss of two company commanders, both with children and wonderful young wives waiting at home, supporting their every need in this war, and looking after other Soldiers' spouses, even in their sadness over the loss of their own husbands.

I took it hard, to say the least. Any time one of my great Soldiers gave his life for the purpose of a better tomorrow, I truly mourned his ultimate sacrifice.

Because we continued to attack the enemy in hopes of that brighter tomorrow, we were not discouraged whatsoever. Most of my Soldiers merely saw the loss of these great Americans as part of God's plan to continue the fight. We, of course, often question why. However, as Soldiers and Americans, we have to understand that there is a greater purpose and believe that we will be successful in all that we do.

We have a great country, but many individuals wanted to continue to make life tough for the Iraqi people through the killing of innocent children and Iraqis who only wanted their god to allow them the opportunity for another tomorrow. They lived for tomorrow, they celebrated life, and they cherished it. They continued to celebrate birthdays, holidays and even weddings with joy and enthusiasm, as if there were no war. During those years, I learned a lot about the customs of the people for whom we were trying to provide some constructive organization and a democratic environment. They were, for the most part, looking forward to the opportunity to have a peaceful country. Some of them saw what Kuwait is now and credit that to the United States Army. I would say we provided the basics of a peaceful environment and they provided the will to develop and maintain it.

During those years, we watched the news, just as you did in the States. We saw our brothers in the Marines being killed, and we watched as their families were interviewed. Most of them said what we all really think.

It was not Iraq that we were fighting anymore. I drove all over this country and saw barefoot kids waving and smiling. I saw men and women daring to show a broken smile and hoping that the insurgents were not around.

I wondered which country we would next try to help to see the error in their ways. The Iraqi Soldiers told me time and time again that they would go with the American Army to any country to fight beside them. This is a great compliment to our Soldiers as well as to all Americans.

After being a part of this operation in Iraq for nearly three years, I found myself considered the resident expert about a lot of things. The day to day "business as usual" for me was different from that of those around me.

As the heat started to rise in May, 2005, the Soldiers who stopped to talk would almost always begin their conversation with, "CSM, it sure is hot."

Nearly always, my reply was, "Soldier, you had better be drinking water. It's not hot yet."

Having been in Iraq during the previous two summers, I knew that the heat would come in August, and then it would turn cold in

September. As in our country, Iraq has its own consistent weather pattern.

When election time came, it presented another situation with which I was familiar. At that time, we, the coalition forces, had to put up the strongest level of security that anyone there had ever seen. I knew we would be burying some Americans because of the increased security and the enemy's increased determination to have the election and our efforts fail. During this time and the following months, the Soldiers experienced the challenges of a lifetime. Still, I could see the way ahead and the light at the end of the tunnel.

Americans other than Soldiers were dying in Iraq. Carl Carroll, a retired Chief Warrant Officer 4 who was working for the Titan Company, was killed after departing my FOB to go to Baghdad. This was and remains a tough thing for me to swallow. Many Americans do not realize that we service members cannot do our job without the support of the Titan Companies and the Halliburtons. They have given us a quality of life that was unheard of in previous wars. There are service members who still do not realize that their fellow veterans who served before them did not have these luxuries. I, for one, appreciate all Americans who have volunteered to come into harm's way and support our troops. Perhaps that is why I became so upset over the lady who, because she had lost a son in war, continued to attack the President in his home town and other places. I wanted her to know that I also feel the pain of a lost Soldier. I have now personally experienced the loss of 34 Soldiers and one civilian from my assigned units. I agree that she is an American. She does have the right to speak out. This is how the backlash of the Vietnam War started. However, over 2,000 service members in the Coalition have lost their lives to support the establishment of freedom in this country. She needs to look at American history and think before she reacts. Thousands and thousands of families lost their fathers and sons during past wars. Their sacrifice has made our country the best nation in this world. I beg her to remember her son for what he did and honor him by letting him rest in peace.

I had become very close to Carl Carroll, a retired aviation veteran who, as a civilian, had come to Iraq to assist us. One morning I heard a loud explosion in the area outside of the FOB. I immediately contacted the Tactical Operation Center to ask them what was going own. They responded that the Special Forces patrol had been hit with an IED, and one vehicle was on fire. I went to the TOC for a situation update and learned that one civilian was being brought to our troop medical clinic. I went to the TMC, and when Carl arrived, I watched every second as our great medical staff, led by Dr. Bean, worked diligently to save him. A short time later, they announced that he was gone. I remember, ever so clearly, asking myself that day if I was ready and if I had done everything to ensure my family would be taken care of, if anything happened to me.

Many times before that day I had done hundreds of patrols. When we first arrived in this area, the top three leaders' patrols were hit almost daily with little damage. At one time, the squadron commander asked me to slow down because he needed me.

I answered, "Roger Sir, when you slow down, I will."

He laughed. He was a great ambassador for our Soldiers. His passion for ensuring they were taken care of, as well as maintaining contact with the enemy, left us in great shape for almost 100 days before we lost our first warrior, Pfc. LaWare.

Later, in 2005, I returned home to a huge welcome home party, including the neighbors and my cousins. I was relatively happy. Still, in my stomach I was sick, sick that I had made it through 30 months of combat. Many more had not, and I could see their faces in my mind all the time. I tried hard to stay busy, even cut short my vacation in order to report to my new position as the Brigade Command Sergeant Major for the Basic Combat Training Brigade at Fort Benning, GA. I was excited to share my experiences with Soldiers and leaders to help prepare them for what they would be facing. Colonel Charles W. Durr had interviewed me by phone several months before and had been willing to wait for me to return. As I began my new job, I found myself forgetting about the war unless I met up with friends and fellow warriors or I watched TV. I remember that when I had first arrived, the good commander told me that he'd see me at Building 4. He explained that I'd be spending a lot of time there for briefings, ceremonies and luncheons. I had been given a government vehicle to drive, so

I left about 20 minutes ahead of time in order to reach the meeting early.

Having been a drill sergeant at Fort Benning from 1989-1992, I knew the area well, but some changes had occurred. I left Sand Hill and headed down Dixie Road at Harmony Church and on in towards Building 4. As I cleared the main area and headed down the last straight-away on Dixie Road, gunfire rang out. My heart jumped and I jerked my steering wheel. I quickly pulled myself together when I realized that I had heard sounds from a firing range. I took a deep breath and told myself that I needed to find a new route. As time went on, I also tried constantly changing routines so as not to spend much of my time focusing on the past. I tried to push it away, unless I got emails, letters, or phone calls from old friends or fellow warriors who needed me. When I needed to visit ranges more often, I tried to find times when these Soldiers were not firing. To be honest, there wasn't much I could do to help them or even talk to them when they were engaged.

I talked to the Commander about setting up different venues to see the Soldiers, in briefs. I wanted to stay on top of the training, stay engaged with Soldiers and leaders alike, but minimize my contact with live firing ranges.

Thirty days into my position, I was asked to go to Atlanta for a few days to discuss which task and battle drills should be added or deleted as the Army was preparing a new training project. When the Commander told me this, I looked at him and asked, "Sir, what the hell are warrior task and battle drills?" I had been at war so long that the Army had become smarter and more creative.

I arrived in Atlanta the morning of the meeting. I hated traveling and being alone, so I hadn't wanted to leave the day before. Being alone with time to think had been my worst enemy for several years. It remains that to this day.

I met Colonel Shwedo, the G-3 for the Army Accessions Command, and we talked a minute before the discussions began. I sat patiently as all good CSM's do, listening to each word. I was thinking, "Okay, Genius, where is your combat patch if you know so damn much?"

After a while, it came to me. Our discussion had been about the tasks they thought were important and how we could create what they called white space by eliminating the tasks that weren't important. I started off slowly and said that "call for fire" is important, but not for basic training Soldiers. They immediately became interested. I then stated that crew serve weapons are important also, but unless they're driving down the road engaging targets, then that too is a task for their next duty station. I finally came to the task that weighed heavily on my heart. While I was in combat, my patrol and I frequently came across patrols that had been hit with IED's. It was hard to understand why they didn't know a damn thing about lifesaver task and how to apply the four basic lifesaving measures. One time a patrol was hit as they were escorting a fuel truck to another FOB in our area. We drove up and saw that the rear seat was heavily damaged and a Soldier, bleeding from shrapnel, was lying across the seat. My patrol immediately secured the area and rendered first aid to that Soldier. From that time on, I constantly enforced first aid training for first responders.

Because of my experiences and strong feelings, I emphasized to the listeners that we are very good at taking the fight to the enemy and destroying them at will. However, I insisted that we are a failure at providing the necessary first response first aid to our Soldiers, and that's why so many die of their wounds. COL Shwedo jumped on that idea quickly, and it soon became the theme of TRADOC to ensure that all Soldiers left initial military training as combat lifesavers. It has made a huge difference to date.

The first year at this post went by quickly, and soon I was asked to go to Fort Jackson for a two-week course that was called Pre-command Course for CSM/COL. The Thursday prior to departing for Fort Jackson, I woke up in severe pain. I didn't know what it was. As I did every day, I got up, put on my physical fitness clothes, and headed to work. That morning I just moved a little more slowly. I got to work almost the same time as the Commander did. I was lucky he had not parked at the same time as I did. I moved slowly up the stairs to the office and sat in pain at my desk on the second floor. The good colonel and I ran all the time together. He had become my battle buddy with whom I had shared almost everything in my life, except that I had been diagnosed with PTS. I regret that to this date. He approached my door and invited me to go for a long run. I said that I could not go, and when he left for the run, I went next door to the TMC to see what the hell was going on. They said I had stones in my bladder and they were trying to come out. They sent me to the hospital for an MRI, but when we arrived, I had to go to the restroom first. By the time I got to the MRI, I was already feeling better.

I arrived on Sunday at Fort Jackson, checked in, and went to my room. I had watched TV the day before, seeing what was going on in Iraq and learning how many more troops were dying. That had left a heavy load on my heart before I went to sleep. That night I awoke screaming that I couldn't understand how I had lived and why other young Soldiers had died. I began sleepwalking again; I had to resort to tying my leg to the bed with my boot string to prevent me from going anywhere. Now I have a sleep apnea machine that works similarly because it's strapped to my head and it blows air all night into my nose. It is uncomfortable, but it keeps me alive.

CHAPTER 15

The Help of Continuing Education in My Battle with PTS

I completed my B.S., B.A. and M.B.A. from TUI University after returning from my third tour of combat in November, 2005. PTS is an illness which can occur after a traumatic event such as combat or military exposure, sexual or physical abuse, terrorist attacks, or serious accidents. A serious traumatic event can trigger serious psychological conditions. Because of the constant deployments and harsh battle conditions, PTS is on the rise in the U.S. military at epidemic proportions. The results can be catastrophic. Suicide can be the Soldier's final choice. In particular, many of my Soldiers and I tend to experience feelings of hopelessness about the future, shock, emotional numbness, rapid heartbeat or breathing, and generally an inability to feel happy and relaxed. I am jumpy, easily startled, and often unable to concentrate. While I was a CSM, I battled with headaches, night sweats, and guilt. These battles led me to excessive drinking, but unlike many others, I did not smoke or use illegal drugs. Soldiers with PTS often try to avoid people and avoid places related to trauma. As a Command Sergeant Major of a brigade, I faced all the same problems, and more. The typical symptoms of nervousness, a feeling of helplessness, and fearfulness were evident quickly. But the worst part was the sense of not trusting others and feeling the need to be all-controlling. Obviously, such issues created conflicts. Sleep was difficult, so I constantly felt overtired. Bad dreams and flashbacks contributed to my irritability and general edginess. I got upset or annoyed very easily. This, of course, impacted my general health. There was excessive weight gain, signs of heart disease, high blood pressure, cholesterol issues, and other health problems, all typical of those affected with PTS. Unfortunately, and also quite commonly, there was a divorce after 26 years of marriage. All of this made it a real challenge for me to live and do my job.

For me, going back to school was a fantastic strategy for coping with PTS. Those suffering from PTS need structure and support from family and friends in all parts of their lives. Education provided me the structure needed to kick-start my own life and deal with the loneliness and suicidal thoughts that come as part of the depression and anxiety of PTS. In the beginning, I had tried other courses of action. In 2007, when I started studying for my bachelor's degree at TUI University, I was at my lowest point emotionally. But the requirement to study and do homework gave me plenty of work to do.

When I took a break for about six months after completing my Bachelor's Degree in 2008, I found that I had too much free time. Education coursework had been a great tool to occupy my mind and keep me involved. It had added structure that led me to personal and professional success. Now I needed more education, the fantastic tool that brought balance to my upside down world. As a result of my studies, I am much more confident in everything that I do.

In particular, the distance learning environment, a flexible, no-exam style education with a critical thinking approach, afforded me the opportunity to work at home at my own pace at the proper time for me, emotionally. The structure of reading and research, along with the freedom to explore and think, kept me busy for hours on end, time that would otherwise have been spent less productively, to say the least.

Success in school can lead to real success in life by building confidence, learning skills, and attaining qualifications for future endeavors. For example, after founding Warrior Outreach, Inc. in 2008, I initiated the Wounded Warrior Horsemanship Program at Fort Benning, GA. I serve as a team captain for the "House of Heroes," which helps renovate homes for older veterans. Working in this program provides me the opportunity to speak with Soldiers about their experiences on the front lines. I am able to let them know that they are not alone and that help is available, if they will just reach out.

Some folks would say that I am old school—a tough Soldier who is blunt and intimidating. But like all the CSMs I know, under that tough armor, we are truly kind and caring individuals. Therefore, fighting the good fight myself, the pressure of leadership, the flag-draped coffins, and the fallen Soldiers that I had trained really took their toll. Since my retirement, I have made it my personal mission to talk openly about my personal experience with Post Traumatic Stress and how it affected my Soldiers and me personally. It takes a lot of guts to be a Soldier, but even more to talk directly about its emotional side. Let's help Soldiers understand that continuing education can serve as an essential tool in their recovery from the effects of war.

CHAPTER 16

Accepting the Challenges

In 2008, I met my present wife, Cathy, and I started a new job, looking at training material and determining resources, with Lockheed Martin. Each day I drove to Fort Benning with anxiety, wanting to exceed the requirements and lead others to do so, as well. Having three months of active duty left on terminal leave before my retirement on January 1, 2009, made it tougher than I had expected. Each day as I went to work, I passed by two lieutenants and NCOs who were attending courses in Building 4, East Wing. They didn't know me from Adam. I watched them every day, passed by them, and tried to figure out just where the last 29 years of my life had gone. I thought often about how far I had come and how tough the last five years had been. As time passed, I found it tougher and tougher to go to work and even tougher to drive home. I found myself having to talk to my doctor on a more regular basis, just trying to understand the challenges of transition.

CHAPTER 17

Making a Difference

To my surprise, in March of 2009, former Chief of Staff, General George W. Casey, sent me an email:

"Sam, if you're ever in D.C., give me a call. I would love to sit down with you."

I had heard this type of message before, only to be locked out at the gate and denied entry. This turned out to be much different for me, and I credit this experience for where I am today.

I replied, "Sir, I am coming to D.C. on April 9 for an awards dinner." (It was for the company for which I was working.)

His aide called me back, gave me a time, and scheduled a meeting with me. Imagine—an old veteran sitting down with the top Army leader! When I arrived at the Pentagon, I found a strange security measure. Those who were DA civilians could enter without any problem. However, as a veteran, I had to get a badge and be escorted wherever I went. I was deeply angry about this measure, but considering what had happened in prior years, it was a measure I accepted. Soldiers are looked at differently the moment they get their retirement cards.

I wandered the halls, waiting for the good general who had decided to do some physical fitness training before meeting with me. I walked in on a conversation that provided a really great understanding of the critical decisions that this man had to make every day. He offered me something to drink, and we sat down. I was still in shock that this was even happening, and to say I was at a loss for words is an understatement.

He started the conversation with, "Sam, how are you doing?"

I lied and said, "Doing fine, Sir."

I could see in his eyes that he was worried about me and not buying into my answer, whatsoever. He thanked me for the article I had written for the infantry magazine in 2007.

General Casey already had thoughts about how I could best help the Army. He wanted me to assist in helping leaders understand those who, like me, were suffering from PTS. He said, "Sam, I want you to go out to Fort Leavenworth and talk to all the future battalion commanders and brigade commanders. Help them understand what a Soldier suffering from PTS goes through and how they can recognize the Soldiers who are struggling."

Ironically, that same year I had been asked to speak at the 2009 Suicide Prevention Conference. I knew the biggest challenge to our Army at this time was preventing Soldiers and veterans from taking their own lives.

I immediately said, "Yes, Sir. Just let me know what I need to do and I will, Sir."

During the 30 minute meeting, he introduced me to a new program called Comprehensive Soldier Fitness. He asked if I would take a look at what they were teaching at the University of Pennsylvania and provide feedback on improvements they could make. Finally, he got to the part that intensified my focus.

"Sam, I want you to add resilience to your speech as you travel around among our Army. Go out to the pre-command course at Fort Leavenworth and talk to our future battalion and brigade commanders."

I asked myself, "Do I tell the good general that I know nothing about resilience?"

I decided against that option, chose the easy way out, shook my head, and replied as all good Soldiers do, "Yes, Sir!"

I found that resilience is the process of adapting well in the face of adversity, trauma, tragedy, threats, and all significant sources of stress, such as family and relationship problems, serious health problems, or workplace and financial issues. It involves "bouncing back" from difficult experiences. Research has shown that resilience is ordinary, not extraordinary. People commonly demonstrate resilience. One example is the response of many Americans to the September 11, 2001 terrorist attacks as seen in the efforts of many individuals to re-build their lives.

Being resilient does not mean that a person doesn't experience difficulty or distress. Emotional pain and sadness are common in people who have suffered major adversity or trauma in their lives. In fact, the road to resilience is likely to involve considerable emotional distress. Resilience is not a trait that people either have or do not have. It involves behaviors, thoughts, and actions that can be learned.

General George W. Casey and Samuel M. Rhodes

General Casey and I had a great exchange during that visit. His calm understanding of the Army was notable in his voice and words. For example, over my 29 years of service, I have found that a leader who has the best intentions must sometimes make the best decisions he can, without having all the information he needs for a certain mission. The general clearly understood that.

As I walked out of his office and made my way from the building, I found myself amazed. After twenty-nine years of service, I had finally made it to the Pentagon. One other thing was on my mind: what the hell is resilience? I was dumb as a rock about it. But I had agreed to do something, so I began researching almost as soon as I reached my room. Before too long, I had a great understanding of resilience and how to use it to help myself through some of the challenges that occur with PTS. After studying long and hard, I decided to put something on a card that could help Soldiers, families and veterans. That's how I created the 10 Steps to Building Resilience, which I started using in my speaking engagements.

In August of 2009, General Casey again asked me to attend the upcoming master resilience course at the University of Pennsylvania and provide him with feedback. It was a tough task, but I managed to get a few days off work. However, I had to fund my own way because I was a contractor. You're never received with open arms when you visit as an outsider.

Several folks shared with me: "Let CSM Rhodes see what he wants to see, but don't let him see certain things and then he'll go away."

I've seen this before when doing external evaluations of other units, and the perception is that you're there as a spy and not for the real reason—to help make things much better.

As I sat in and listened to several classes, I found it intriguing. Unfortunately, I could not immediately find the connection with how this could be taught to a platoon of Soldiers. As we broke for lunch, I began talking to several drill sergeants that I recognized from Fort Benning, asking them what they thought of the classes.

One drill sergeant replied, "I can use this immediately to help me!"

That was good. I talked to several more and almost all of them felt that the material they were being taught on resilience was just what the doctor had ordered.

I asked another tough question: "How can you implement this into a platoon structure?"

There was instant silence. One drill sergeant finally said, "I am not sure about that just yet."

I must have talked one-on-one to nearly 50 people, including civilians and spouses, during the days I was there. Every one of them came from a different background. Deputy COL Williams told me that the global assessment tool, the resilience training, and the modules would clearly make a difference, if presented and used correctly.

Cathy and I were on our second visit to D.C. when we had a blessed opportunity to sit down in the conference room of our hotel and just talk with Brigadier General Cornum, who was managing and providing guidance from the Chief of Staff to make this master resilience trainer course come to life. What a vision she had! I was impressed with her words and compassion for the warriors who were challenged. Clearly, General Casey had chosen the best possible general officer to lead this program into the future. I was humbled by her words. She asked me to work with her and her staff to assist in getting the CSF message out.

I asked, "Ma'am, may I use your slide presentation?"

She replied, "Certainly," and I knew by the time she left us that there was more to her than what I had learned from her that day. Here was an Army officer focused on helping others.

Brigadier General Cornum was a prisoner of war during Desert Storm after her helicopter had been shot down. That was the easy part to find out. However, this lady had endured some of the toughest challenges that a Soldier can encounter in combat. What the enemy did to her because she is a woman would have taken the life out of almost anyone else. There is a YouTube video during which she explains to the news media how the sergeant who was captured with her had apologized for not being able to help her when she was screaming from the secured room where the enemy had placed her. He had spent that time blaming himself for what they were doing.

Her response to him after they were released was, "Sergeant, it's not your fight. You had no way to help me. You need to understand that the things that you cannot control, you need to just let go."

WOW! I found those to be great words to live by as my own challenges continued. Yes, I was still struggling. I had not yet mastered control over my anxiety, the guilt for surviving the war, and the stress of not having a job that I could have for the rest of my life. I was fighting to understand that I am normal. Often, as I walked the halls of Fort Benning's offices, I wondered if folks were thinking, "There goes that CSM who has PTS. Stay away from him."

I had this picture in my mind that people were avoiding me; friends who didn't text or email, friends who would see me and keep walking. Others added to my stress because they didn't think I had PTS. Yes, sometimes I just needed to dig really deep and remember that if they were really my friends, they would know.

Speaking out and talking about my challenges helped many people open up to their families, friends, peers, and leaders. I found myself speaking so much at this time that it was having an adverse effect on me. The impact became devastating—restless nights, lack of energy, nightmares. Almost like clockwork, every time I stood in front of an audience discussing what contributes to my PTS, the next couple of days would be hell, and I would often wake up to find Cathy holding me in her arms.

"It will be okay, Baby. It will be okay."

CHAPTER 18

Realizing my Reason for Living

Over the course of the last several years, I have looked at many incidents or situations and asked myself, "If I hadn't done something, what would have happened?" It was that day in June, 2009, that I often wondered about. If I had taken my own life, how would that have affected the outcome of that day?

It was a very beautiful morning when I awoke at seven o'clock and began my day by having breakfast with my wife, Cathy. I prepared to head out to get a few workers to help me repair a fence where I was keeping my horses. Ms. Ann Slaughter had allowed me to board my horses on that property in return for keeping the fences up. I took the 30-minute drive to Columbus to find a few helpers and headed back to her home off Cannon Road in Harris County, just a few miles from my home. I had really grown attached to Ms Ann, as I referred to her. Her husband, John Slaughter, had passed away earlier in the year. I always remind myself during tough times that everything happens for a reason. Nothing occurs without impacting something else in life. I was driving down the road by her property one day and noticed that the fence that bordered her home was falling down. Her property of 12 acres was very nice with plenty of grazing pasture for my three horses. I decided to call her and leave a message, and then I dropped by to introduce myself. I was intrigued by her beautiful personality. Like most women who reach the age of seventy, she greeted me with a warm smile and a gentle hug. Yes,

I have been called a hugger, but that's one of the nice things I have been called. These days I get about as many Happy Mother's Day calls as I get Happy Father's Day calls; go figure. Ms Ann Slaughter is the grandmother that I never had while I was growing up. She has a warm personality, a soft voice, and the most beautiful smile. I knew instantly this was a terrific lady. I asked her if she would rent her pasture out to me to board a couple horses. When she replied that her fence probably would not hold the horses, I stated I would be more than glad to fix it for her if we could work out something. She agreed. The next day was Saturday, so I got up early on my own to start repairing the fence. About two hours into fixing the fence it started raining really hard. I kept working. Butch, her nephew, came out to ask if I wanted to come in to the dry area. I thanked him and continued to work. An hour or so later it stopped raining and the most beautiful rainbow appeared. It was now a beautiful day.

One day, the work was too much for me, so I enlisted some helpers to help me put a big dent into it. We arrived around 9 AM and started working, removing weeds, tree limbs, and other stuff in preparation to repair the fence. About three hours later, my wonderful wife, Cathy, brought us our lunch. After lunch, we worked for a few more hours. It was about 3:45PM when I called it a day, and we drove down to the local fuel tech to see if I could get some cash out of the ATM to pay my workers. For some reason the ATM didn't work for me.

I decided to drive back towards my home to the hardware store to see if Mr. Wilson could give me some cash through his machine. I was able to get some cash and off I went. Little did I realize the importance of this eight to ten minute delay. After talking to the workers and thanking them for all their help, I drove towards Columbus. Suddenly I noticed that traffic ahead had stopped. I continued up the road and saw a minivan sitting at the bottom of a steep slope with the air bag deployed. I immediately jumped out and ran down the bank to the van.

As I got closer to the vehicle it became obvious to me that it was the vehicle of our friend, Cindy Jo. I looked inside and I couldn't see anything. I snatched the driver's side door open and looked inside. To my surprise, a body was lying across both seats with most of it underneath the dash board and glove box. I regained my composure and started to give aid to the victim. I pulled her head and upper torso out from under the dash and observed that her airway was obstructed with a large amount of blood. Her eyes were rolled back and she was unconscious. I started yelling at her, and when I got her all the way to a sitting position, I began to rub her face gently to get her to recognize me and hear me tell her that she was going to be okay. She opened her eyes and asked who I was. When I told her I was Sam, Cathy's husband, she said she didn't know me. She began to roll her eyes back again, and I screamed louder, telling her to stay with me. I was still yelling and screaming for help when a local Columbus police officer arrived at the scene.

The police officer asked me if I thought she was going to be okay. I grabbed my phone and hit speed dial for my stepson, Jason Martin, a fireman on duty at his station in Columbus. I told the officer to tell Jason where we were and what we needed. I wanted them to come quickly and assist me in stabilizing Cindy Jo. She was telling me that she couldn't breathe, and then she began hyperventilating. I placed my hand by her mouth and told her to breathe slowly. She responded, but she was in a lot of pain.

I yelled again for someone to open the passenger's side door so that we could have fresh air blowing through the vehicle to help Cindy Jo breathe and maybe relax. As I stabilized her, I continued to fight with her to keep her conscious until the EMS arrived. When they arrived, I briefed them on the situation and her status. I told them that I had checked for any obvious external damage, and that the only apparent injuries were to her face. I informed them that she had been unconscious when I arrived, I was able to get her up, and she regained consciousness but slipped in and out of it. I helped them to secure her with a neck brace as well as a back brace and then carry her up the hill. I provided them with her purse so that they would have identification. After EMS departed for the medical center, I approached the fire truck to see if I could get some sanitizing liquid to get the blood off my hands and shoulders. By this time I had contacted my wife, Cathy, and she knew that I was fighting hard to handle this situation. I had seen this far too often in Iraq when I had come upon injured Soldiers and civilians and rendered aid. It is a constant reminder to me that life is so fragile. I tried to sleep Saturday night, but I kept recalling the vision of our friend. Who wants to arrive on a scene and find a close friend in such bad shape? I was awake most of the night, thinking only about going to the hospital and seeing Cindy Jo.

Cathy and I awoke early Sunday. We tried to relax and watch a movie. She fell back asleep in my arms and the movie ended around 11 o'clock. She kept rubbing my hand in a motion similar to what I had done for Cindy. It seemed as if she knew what I needed to do. She asked if I wanted to go to see Cindy, and then we dressed and headed to the medical center. Visiting hours started at noon, so we headed right up to the 8th floor ICU and proceeded to bed 10.

The head nurse stopped us as we entered the room to let us know she had just given Cindy some sleeping medicine for her intense pain. I asked softly for permission to just go into the room. Cathy stayed by the nurse, and I went over to Cindy's bed and began rubbing her right hand. Amazingly, Cindy Jo whispered, "That feels so good. That feels so good."

I spoke softly so as not to startle her, and I asked if she knew me.

She began to cry, and then she said, "Sam, I love you. You saved my life. I remember you yelling my name and telling me to stay with you. Sam, you're my angel. God sent you to Cathy and now to me. I could see the light; I was headed home. You didn't let me go; you saved my life."

She kept repeating those words. When my wife walked into the room, I told Cindy that Cathy was there with us. She started crying more, repeating to Cathy how lucky they both were that I was an angel for them, and how she owed me her life.

The emotional stress on me at that point was overwhelming, but I remained calm, kissed Cindy on the forehead, and assured her that we both loved her. I asked her to rest and promised that I'd come back. As we walked down the hall to the elevator, Cathy recognized that I was being overwhelmed again. At the elevator, she gave me a hug and told me she loved me. When we began our drive home, she asked in a soft, crying voice if I was okay.

I thought for a second, and then I replied, "God must be punishing me. Surely he knows what seeing this over and over again does to me."

She answered, "Everything happens for a reason. God let you survive the war because he had more for you to do. Today he wanted you to save Cindy Jo."

I hadn't thought of it like that. I spent the rest of the day with friends and family trying to relax and enjoy them. Frequently I thought about Cindy Jo, wondering if she was okay. Often I would remember the events in Iraq that were so similar, and I would drift off to be by myself. Cathy would come to find me and pull me back in.

I have wrestled so much with the death of friends, fellow warriors and even strangers. Is it my purpose to help others through difficult times as God has helped me? I believe it is. I had pledged my life months ago to help others. This weekend reinforced that pledge. I am still here for a reason, and on this particular day, the reason was to be an angel for Cindy Jo. So whenever you have that thought about ending all your troubles, close your eyes and think carefully. Realize that it's really not just about *you*. How many people's lives will change for the worse because of your poor judgment? I asked myself if I really wanted my grandson to use me as a role model. If he goes through some challenging, painful times, do I want him to think that if it was good enough for his Papa, it's good enough for him? Bang . . . No! Let me share a message from Cindy Jo:

My name is Cindy Jo Cato. The story above was about my horrific accident on June 9, 2009. It was my best friend, Sandra's, birthday. I was headed home in the middle of the afternoon to prepare for a birthday dinner out with the girls. I never made it. I rounded a sharp curve in the road and realized that the white truck in front of me was not moving, and he had no tail lights on to warn me. I grabbed the steering wheel and overcompensated, projecting myself into a ravine, through a fence, into a telephone pole, coming to rest against a tree. All I remember is terrible pain—the worst pain I have ever felt. I couldn't breathe. I remember opening my eyes and seeing blood dripping off my face. My upper torso felt as if it was crushed. I looked up and said, "God, I can't do this."

At that point I was surrounded by a white light. It was the most peaceful, quiet place. I had no pain and I could breathe. I knew I was going home.

All of a sudden I heard a voice, "Cindy Jo, don't leave me. Cindy Jo, I've got you; don't leave me".

God had sent me an angel. He was not ready for me yet. Command Sergeant Major Samuel M. Rhodes was my angel. If it had not been for Sam's ATM mishaps that day, I would not be here. Yes, Sam, everything does happen for a reason. Had you committed suicide during your dark hour, I would not be here to live life to the fullest as I do. I thank God for having you there for me at that time. He knew you would touch lives in a way most people never can. Every day that I get to be with my children, my grandchildren, my friends, and my patients is possible because God did not allow you to take your own life. If just one person who is contemplating suicide is swayed by reading this, I thank you, Jesus, and I thank you, Sam, for sharing your experiences in an effort to help others in similar situations. Every person on the face of God's earth is here for a reason. Sometimes it takes soul searching to figure it out but it's worth the effort. Have faith that you are here for a reason, and realize that there are people whose lives will suffer tremendously, picking up the pieces after their loved ones commit such an act. I experienced that devastation after my brother took his own life in 2004. I saw the pain in his children's eyes and still see it to this day. Thank you, Sam Rhodes. I owe you my life and I thank God for yours.

CHAPTER 19

Knowing I Mattered

I thought long and hard about all the blessings that came in 2010 to the Rhodes family. In January, I gave 14 presentations across the country. In the middle of the month, Cathy and I traveled to Fort Campbell, KY, to provide some Post Traumatic Stress awareness briefings to a brigade that was deploying. Using my own experiences, I certainly considered this event to be one of the highlights of the year. I remember seeing an SFC with his sunglasses on sitting in the lobby, and I walked up to him to say hello. After I gave the presentation, as always, I hung around talking with Soldiers, families and leaders and exchanging email addresses. The SFC, so quiet before, walked up to Cathy and me. I was stunned at his comments.

"I am sorry, Command Sergeant Major. I was rude to you when you walked up to me in the lobby, and I did exactly the thing you're trying to stop. I stigmatized you as someone who was going to present just another boring, non-caring briefing about PTS. I was wrong. I think there is hope. Your message about helping ourselves really hit home with me. I am going to work harder than ever before to help myself. I never looked at the entire picture and realized that leaders, themselves, are overwhelmed with the war, the day to day activities, priorities, and caring for us."

We left Fort Campbell with a good feeling about their program and what they were doing to get Soldiers to help themselves during the toughest time of their lives.

On January 21, 2010, I found myself in Fort Jackson, South Carolina, talking to another group in an NCO leadership course; it would prove to be a blessing. As I walked in, I was met by several Soldiers with whom I had served during my military career and who were taking the course. It remains a blessing to have seen the growth of these Soldiers in their lives and in their commitment to the Army. As I talked to these NCOs, I found myself working with a different kind of group. Usually a 90-minute presentation would come and go, with several Soldiers talking after, but never during, the presentation. This time it was different. I engaged the audience and asked tough questions.

"As a leader, what do you think we should do with Soldiers who come forward and ask for help?"

One NCO stood up and said, "I think he needs to take a knee, allow himself to recover, and get back in the fight."

A female NCO stood up and offered, "I think we need to accept the challenge and allow that Soldier to go for help and remain with the unit."

Finally, I got the answer I was looking for: "The norm of the Army is to call you weak if you ask for help. I had an NCO tell his platoon sergeant that he wanted to get help and immediately he singled him out. He sent him to see the First Sergeant and afterwards both sergeants laughed about it. That Soldier ended up in a warrior transition battalion. I don't want to be that Soldier."

Yes, that is the typical story across our Army. We want to reduce stigma, but we don't want PTS sufferers in our unit. Warrior transition battalions are an excellent tool, but they're not the only tool. We have to be willing to accept the idea that this Soldier was good enough to deploy with me, kick down a door in a four-man stake, and come home. We cannot decide that we don't want him around if he has issues.

After I made these same comments, I could sense the feeling in the room. Many were wondering if they were hearing me correctly. Yes, I have found that part of coping is providing structure in your life so that you understand everything. A Soldier, family member, or veteran suffering from PTS doesn't wake up in the morning and say, "I want to be angry today, and I want to hate the world. I want everyone to look at me as if I am weak because what I did or saw in the war bothers me."

Death, destruction and life have a way of doing just that.

On the drive home, I did a lot of thinking. I wondered if anyone got the message or if I did help one person. Yes, I believe I did. The emails from that presentation alone have me communicating with Iowa National Guard and other Guard organizations. The message is growing. JUST CARE!

On January 29, 2010, I was in Boston, Massachusetts, on the coldest day of the year. The Blue Star Moms of Massachusetts had recruited us to come to speak to their organization and the surrounding community. Just as happens during most of the presentations, Cathy and I received much more than we could have ever given. We met the chapter's vice president and her son, who is a veteran 100% disabled with PTS from OIF. Like all of us who suffer from PTS, he faces quite a challenge. We are so uncomfortable with ourselves, and our anxiety, stress and depression seem to be as much a part of our lives as waking up in the morning. I talked with her son several times that weekend and many times since. He remains hopeful that he can maintain a level head and a positive attitude despite the fact that it seems as if someone is there trying to knock him down at every turn.

Soldiers, veterans and family members who have spoken to me one-on-one over the last several years continue to just want peace. Yes, it's that simple—peace to forget the memories of those who never came home, peace to forget the self-imposed guilt of returning home alive, peace to stop the dreams that are triggered by the smallest obstacle, peace from the anger inside over the fact that most people do not care. Yes, like Jared, I too have built some security in believing that the positive opinions of others matter very much and give us balance. On the other hand, when we get the feeling that a peer, a friend, a supervisor or even a family member sees us in any light other than a positive one, it gives us a negative indication that our value is decreased. Yes, opinions that others have of us affect our own ability to cope with the stresses of life. During most of my presentations, I talk about keeping things in perspective. Change is a part of life that takes care of you. It is a part of building the resiliency and stamina that one needs.

I did four presentations in Massachusetts over a four-day period. I got the opportunity to talk to mothers whose sons will never come home, to parents whose sons are 100% disabled and angry at the world, and to veterans who would have nowhere to go, were it not for a homeless shelter. It was an amazing trip, and I learned so much. I walked away with a humbled heart. I had never worn a pair of shoes like those of these mothers and fathers. When I lace up my shoes in the morning, the experience I have would frighten most. When I left Massachusetts my shoe laces were a little tighter. Never having experienced the death by suicide of a family member, I left that day with a new perspective. I had thought about suicide in April, 2007. It had been a close call for me. Now I understand what happens to his family when a Soldier takes his own life. I now know how that act hurts the family for the rest of their lives! The mothers I talked with ask themselves every day what else they could have done and why they failed. Tough thoughts, for certain!

The month of February proved to be even tougher than January. I found myself scheduling more events, wanting to just help. As I read an email from the Vice Chief of Staff of the Army, it tugged on my heart. It tugged so much that I included this quote from him in my presentation:

> "At the end of the day, no matter how much effort we spend on programs, how many changes we make to policies, or how many hours we spend on suicide prevention training, our last and most potent line of defense remains our leadership."—VCSA Gen. Chiarelli, January, 2010.

We held our 2nd Annual Wounded Warrior Horsemanship event at Ft. Benning on February 6, 2010. Each event had expanded. I had now enlisted the Morale Support Activity Directorate at Benning to assist in providing minimum support for an event designed to give Soldiers, veterans and their families a much needed avenue or structure to help them adapt to life. That day turned out to be cold, but the smiles and the thoughts of the Soldiers and their families would warm the coldest heart of any person. Soldiers, families and veterans enjoyed four hours of learning about horses from students from the tri-city area of Hamilton, Georgia, Phenix City, Alabama, and Seale, Alabama. These students are the heart of the program. Were it not for their volunteering, this program would never have gotten off the ground.

One day, I received a short notice call from COL Charlie Jones, the J1 from the Kentucky Guard.

I realized that I was in trouble when he spoke the first words, "Sam, can you help a brother out?" I paused for a moment and laughed.

He explained, "We're having the Kentucky Guard Conference here in Lexington, Kentucky. Do you want to come to speak?"

Charlie and I go back several years. We had served together and stayed in touch, even at the end of my first tour when he reached out to me for some advice while he was preparing his brigade for deployment. This would be the first time I'd seen Charlie since I had gone to his son's funeral when he died in Iraq in 2006. That's a lot of time between friends, for sure. When I arrived at his hotel, I was eager to see Charlie, and I finally found him on the second floor, going from one hospitality room to the other, visiting with his troops. We embraced as if we hadn't seen each other in a life time; it seemed to have been that long, though we had corresponded often. I didn't know what I was up against that weekend until later that night. Charlie and I walked around as he introduced me to one officer after another.

Each of them said the same thing, "I heard so much about you. Welcome, brother."

I felt really at home. Cathy and I had brought along with us a Kentucky guardsman whom I had served with in 2001 and who had retired several years back. He was a legacy.

I remember the General Officer coming up to him and grabbing him, as he said, "Ben, I remember you; you enlisted me back in 1977."

What a memory! That would be the tone for the night. Finally, as we visited all the hospitality rooms, we engaged with a lot of Soldiers who knew firsthand what the cost of war had been for the state of Kentucky. They shared many a story. The one that touched my heart was about Charlie. He was still deployed when his son died in Iraq. If there is something worse than that, it's being 10 miles away and not able to do anything. Charlie and his son had both deployed together. They both wanted to serve their country. Again I found myself in shoes that didn't fit just right. I had never experienced what a mother, dad, brother or sister felt when their loved one deployed for war. Now the shoes were getting even bigger, as I began to understand how strong a man Charlie Jones really was.

The officer asked me, "How did he do it? How was he able to redeploy to fight in a war that had taken his son away from him?"

I was speechless; at a loss for words was an understatement.

I finally said, "He loves his son, he loves this country, and he is one committed leader I would follow anywhere."

The next day I gave my presentation to about 750 officers from the Kentucky Guard. The emotion and enthusiasm ran high, and the hour went by fast, as I engaged the leadership of this great state's Guard forces. To a leader, I could see that they got the message that we can't forget our Soldiers, families and veterans when they come home or even when they demobilize them. The National Guard has the biggest challenge because they are so far apart from each other. One Guard officer said that he lived outside of Chattanooga. That's a long way to travel, indeed, to serve your country and your state. We spent that evening in a good old fashioned southern family reunion. Though we are not related to any of these officers and Soldiers, we became an instant part of the family. At every turn, someone had something positive to say or a story to tell about what they or their Soldiers were going through. In the bathroom, a wife asked Cathy how I was doing. The lady thought I seemed so focused. Cathy told her that I have good days and bad days, and that we battle this thing together. She admitted that just a few months ago I had considered taking my own life again. Cathy advised the wife to just listen, accept that her husband is different, and hold him as often as possible to remind him that she loves him. WOW! Words like this guided me in 2010, but certainly Cathy hit the nail on the head when she explained that it's a daily battle with the struggles of PTS issues.

You see, I never talk about this, but every time, prior to the days I am going to speak, I wonder if there is someone whom I am going to help. After the speech, I ask myself if I said the right things. I am looking for that 100% solution to helping Soldiers. As the anxiety builds, I begin to speak and engage my thoughts during the presentation. Even when I talk one on one, I am reliving the experiences of the past, each and every opportunity that I get. The last night in the hotel In Kentucky, Cathy found herself, as she has done on so many occasions, grabbing me, holding me, kissing me on the forehead, and telling me that it was going to be fine and that I was okay.

Yes, I still dream; dreams are a product of the triggers that I have allowed myself to engage in during so many events and in so many conversations. Because that happens so much now, I find myself battling my nerves daily. As we traveled home, I realized that it had been a long night. Cathy seemed quiet, and finally she spoke up, asking me what I thought of the trip.

I told her, "It was great to see COL Charlie Jones. I really enjoyed it. Why?"

She answered, "Seems like over the last couple years, each time you speak you go back into depression. Are you doing okay? When is your next appointment?"

I told her when my next appointment was, and she volunteered to go with me, as always. I don't think I ever answered that other question, but I should have. Yes, it hurts to think about the servicemen in combat. It hurts even worse to hear that these warriors have come back to a welcome home banner, still feeling that society hasn't accepted them. Since April, 2009, when I met with Chief of Staff of the Army, General Casey, I have placed emphasis on being resilient. Sometimes it's easier said than done.

It was not easy after meeting with General Casey. New pressure to help others mounted at every turn. I struggled at times, because the lingering thoughts of suicide return more often than one wants to admit. The challenges of telling others how weak you get are almost insurmountable. However, the passion for life and the understanding of it have enabled me to survive thus far. The battle will continue. I need only to believe in and build psychological resilience to prepare myself for those tough days.

There were tough days when I felt guilty because my niece's husband, Darrel, had lost his legs from eating oysters during a family vacation. On another occasion, I was overwhelmed financially when I found out just how much it cost to take care of a horse whose eye had become infected while we were away. I asked myself over and over again if my niece and Darrel would have gone on that vacation had we not gone. If I had been here, perhaps I could have caught the horse's eye infection earlier and the treatment and recovery would have been quicker. As I was asking myself those things, I found out that my only son, who had been out of the Army for three years, was recalled from the inactive to the ready Reserve. Though I support the Army at war, I had anxiety about sending my only son into combat. Just a day later, I learned that my former spouse had suffered a heart attack and been air-evacuated to the University of Alabama Medical Center. I was torn between concern for her well being and the challenges that come for me each and every day.

On August 5, 2009, I was so overwhelmed with anxiety that it led me to a depressive state in which I almost convinced myself that it would be easier to say good bye than to live. As I thought longer about it, I heard my own words, the ones that I use when I speak across the country. I told myself I was a coward, and I asked myself what I was thinking. What about Jeffery, Jordan, Tanner, Kristopher, Liana, Jalen, and Kason? They would miss Papa. I thought about Amiee, Amanda, Sam, Kaitlynn, Kristi, Jason, and Kenny, my nephew, whom I put through high school. I considered my friends who always observed when I was struggling and made sure they'd be there for me. Most of all, I thought about the huge sacrifice that Cathy had made for me. Yes, it's apparent that these thoughts never wander far away, but it's good to have psychological resilience to help when you need it most.

By talking to others and sharing my story, I have singlehandedly improved my own desire to succeed and overcome. I am no role model, just an everyday Soldier who struggles on a daily basis. Am I more receptive to harming myself as I battle through PTS now that I have deployed and returned to our great country? Yes, but with the level of support available, it's an inspiration to help others and that helps me.

CHAPTER 20

Losing a Fellow Brother in Arms

In my last book, I questioned the purpose of Veterans Day. I thought about that as a theme for this new book. I was celebrating life and family on a trip to Las Vegas to see my son, his wife, and my wonderful granddaughters. While there, we learned of the death of my former CSM. Now I found myself less interested in the family celebration and more focused on how I would get to the funeral to celebrate the life and death of CSM Charles P. Cox. When I arrived, I talked with his family about all the things that he and I had shared during my assignment and deployment with him. Never was I more disappointed at a funeral with full military honors than at his funeral. Cathy and I had driven 500 miles to Titusville, FL, to be with his mom, daughter, son and other family members at the viewing being held from 6 PM-8 PM. I was very touched by his personal video that they were showing on a screen in the foyer of the funeral parlor. I knew that this funeral was going to be a challenge for me. However, I felt that I had prepared myself better than ever. Since Charles's death I had been focusing on the positives that we had accomplished together. I remembered the five months we had spent in Kuwait in 1996 away from our families. We had shared a tent for most of that tour. As I watched the video of his Army service, I was drawn to his combat patch. It was the same as mine. I had never known that he, too, was an Eagle Horse Soldier. As I read the program for his service, I found nothing in it that tied him to any unit. I was disappointed, to say the least.

That night I got on the computer and googled the message he had sent to the Eagle Horse:

> *Salutations and Greetings, Fellow Troopers: I served two tours in the Eagle Horse: 1976 to 1980 as a gunner and tank commander in H Company and Fox Troop, and 1989 to 1993 as Gator Troop First Sergeant. I retired as Command Sergeant Major of 1-64 Armor in Ft Stewart in 1997. My proudest and most favorite time in the Army, however, was the time I spent in the Blackhorse. The troopers were the best I ever served with anywhere in the Army. I look forward to hearing from my old friends and Soldiers.*

CSM Charles P. Cox had been battling cancer for several months prior to this message. At the peak of his battle with cancer, he had still found time to reach out to his fellow veterans.

The next day I had breakfast with the Cox family and their friends. Along with the good food, we enjoyed each other's company and shared our individual memories of Charles. Yes, we all seemed to be ready to attend the funeral and begin celebrating the life of a father, son, brother, Soldier and combat veteran whom each of us knew in his/her own special way.

The service at the chapel went well as most do, and I was again extremely happy that I remained resilient and focused. The road trip to the cemetery went really fast as the local motorcycle group, signifying their support for this veteran, made a path for us. There were some challenging moments for me, when I watched the eight-man detail take Charles's casket out of the hearse and place it in its final resting place. The pastor read a psalm and then asked me to come forward to read a note from the FORSCOM Commander who had served with Charles and me as the BDE Commander when we were at Fort Stewart.

It was a powerful letter coming from a Four-Star General. Today, his type of compassion is seldom found in the leadership that surrounds Soldiers. Yes, it's true that not all leaders can find compassion; they look for strength to survive and to be an inspiration. As they take their warriors again and again into harm's way, it's never good to appear weak. When the funeral detail retrieved the weapons from the stack arms position, I was shocked to see that only five weapons were going to be fired. I was so overwhelmed by this, that I almost forgot to salute as they fired the first volley. By the end of the three volleys, I realized that this honors ceremony had left my friend six rounds short of what he should have received. The service ended and I approached the NCOIC for the burial detail. He immediately recognized me as a former CSM and said hello. When I asked him what had happened with the detail, he quietly explained that his unit was tasked out and he was told to do the best he could with what he had.

WOW! Join the Army, defend your country at every turn, and be forgotten when you are gone! Yes, that is how I felt that day when my friend was honored. I thought then about all the other veterans. Has our country forgotten their sacrifice or has our Army become too busy to appreciate those that went before us? As a nation, we ask Soldiers to sacrifice their freedom, their livelihood and even their lives. What do they ask for in return? They expect full military honors when they depart this world, either by natural causes or by the hands of the enemy. I hope we regain the understanding of their service and take the extra step to honor those who laid the framework for us.

Searching the internet, I found thousands of words about veterans and ways to honor them after they are gone, but none were more important than those of our former President:

THE WHITE HOUSE OFFICE
October 8, 1954

I have today signed a proclamation calling upon all of our citizens to observe Thursday, November 11, 1954 as Veterans Day. It is my earnest hope that all veterans, their organizations, and the entire citizenry will join hands to ensure proper and widespread observance of this day. With the thought that it will be most helpful to coordinate the planning, I am suggesting the formation of a Veterans Day National Committee . . . . I am requesting the heads of all departments and agencies of the Executive branch to assist the Committee in its work in every way possible.

I have every confidence that our nation will respond wholeheartedly in the appropriate observance of Veterans Day, 1954.

Sincerely,
DWIGHT D. EISENHOWER

Yes, it was the earnest hope of Dwight D. Eisenhower that our nation would respond wholeheartedly in the observance of Veterans Day. They have, but is it enough?

For the last several years, I have attended a Veterans Day event at the school of my grandson, Tanner Martin, who was in first grade when I was first honored by an invitation to come to eat lunch with his class. I was amazed that a small town school in rural Fortson, Georgia, would ask a veteran to come to lunch. I arrived an hour early as all good Soldiers should. As I approached the school, my throat tightened and I could feel the anxiety to cry. No, I wasn't unhappy; I was overjoyed. I entered the building and met a receptionist who gave me a name tag that said "Happy Veterans Day." It was already a wonderful one, but I didn't realize how wonderful it would become.

I was directed to Tanner's class to meet his teacher, Ms. Ellis. When I entered the classroom, I remembered how much I had enjoyed the younger days of my schooling. (NOT!) I informed Ms. Ellis that I had brought a bag of candy, some American flags, a wrist band with the word HOOAH on it, and some other items for the kids. They were told not to open the bag until after the reading period which was coming up next. I went with four kids to another classroom where Mrs. Pate had us all sit on the floor in a circle. I learned that the students always read for about 30 minutes before they went to lunch. I sat quietly, watching the teacher interact with about 15 kids. All of them were reading, and all were excited about answering the questions about the story. I was amazed that when the teacher got to the part about how animals camouflaged themselves in order to survive in their environment, I became the center of attention!

Ms. Ellis said, "You see Tanner's grandfather's uniform?"

They all said in harmony, "Yes."

When she asked what color it was, they answered, "Brown!"

"Where would you use that color if you wanted to hide from your enemies?" she asked.

They all said, so smartly, "The desert."

I was getting involved; I thought maybe I was supposed to be reading too! Reading time flew by very quickly. Before I knew it, I was back in the classroom posing for photos with the kids and taking the opportunity to talk about some tokens that I had brought to share. I showed the class the dog tags that I had worn in Iraq for over 30 months, during three tours of combat. The children asked many questions, some more direct than others.

Then it was time to open the packs of goodies that I had brought for them. I was wondering what they would pull out first. I should have guessed! It was the small 1"x2" American flag that they all pulled out first. I had to get a photo. Then I was amazed again when they yelled out, "USA!" Truly this Veterans Day was a blessing. After finishing with the bag, we headed to lunch, and all the kids were trying to figure out how to sit with Tanner and his grandfather. They had plenty of questions, and all of them seemed to need me to open something for them. I was sure that they could have handled it themselves, but I opened milk cartons, snacks, and even some frozen peaches.

We spent about 30 minutes together at lunch and we had a great time. One boy told me that his mom was in the Army. Another one told me his grandfather was a Soldier who had died last year. Finally, the best part was when two boys and a little girl said that they were going to be Soldiers. I smiled, hoping that they would give their education a chance first. All in all, it was a truly great Veterans Day for me.

So, have we accomplished what former President Dwight D. Eisenhower wanted for Veterans Day? Do you think we have? Unfortunately, across the country, the kids still have to go to school rather than spend the day with their Veteran.

The best message I ever got on a Veterans Day came from my wife, Cathy. It was a great explanation of her feelings, and it brought tears to my eyes:

I am sorry that I didn't realize what you felt. I do not understand why you did not express these feelings to me when I asked you how the lunch with Tanner went. Why don't you talk openly to me anymore? I now know that you are disappointed in me for not making a point of celebrating Veterans Day. I should have had the family over for a cookout or just dinner. I am truly sorry. I am so proud of you, my husband, and all that you have done to accomplish such a great career in the Army. As I looked at the video the other day of your family celebrating with you, I realized that I do not honor you as they did and I know that you miss that celebration. But I cannot read your mind. You have to plan those celebrations with me. The Army has been such a part of your life that I do not understand completely as your old family did. You have to work with me for these important days. I am happy that you had Tanner to make your day better. We have a lot of issues going on right now in our lives, but you have to talk to me about the good and the bad. I know that you are a wonderful husband and are always looking out for our best interest and I love you very much for that.

Just remember the most important thing!!! I love you with all my heart forever, and I want you to be happy with your new life as a civilian and mostly as my partner.

All my love, forever,
Cathy

CHAPTER 21

Using the Love of Family to Recharge

I have made fewer speaking engagements since I took on my new government position with the Army. In 2010, I became the Program Manager for Comprehensive Soldier and Family Fitness. I had spoken so often in so many places—occasionally, five or six times in one day—from 2008-2010, that I actually found myself physically and mentally exhausted. Those years taught me the meaning of resilience. I had to find some other way to help Soldiers without reliving countless memories that caused me more pain than most folks could ever imagine. Horrific memories can assault the mind when you least expect it. When talking about my combat experiences, even the smell of battle came back. Sights and sounds exploded in my thoughts. Talking about Post Traumatic Stress helps with the healing process. But there comes a time when you need to put it behind you. A time comes when you realize that you will not let PTS define your life. Turning the page on PTS does not mean forgetting your combat experience. For me, it meant realizing that although I received excellent help from the mental health professionals, helping myself is a priority. The best medicine for dulling the bad memories is "friends and family." Taking time to soak in their love helped inoculate me from the past. I took a few months off from my speaking engagements to reflect on the true meaning of life and contemplate the great adventures that are still ahead. Now I'm ready to charge back into the arena with a renewed vigor. My calling is "helping Soldiers." Now that I'm rested, I'm back.

These are the words of a close friend:

Over the last several years, I could see that each time Sam spoke to an audience about his struggles with PTS a heavy toll was taken on his mental and physical health. The more he tried to help others, the more weight seemed to be on his shoulders. He needed a break. He needed to reexamine his priorities. Since his sabbatical, I've seen a new Sam. He is now rested and confident. He has a new sense of purpose. Helping Soldiers is in Sam's blood, but he needs to help himself first. Sometimes you just need to gather your loved ones around you and relax.

CHAPTER 22

Walking in the Shoes of Others

If I have learned one thing in the past seven years, it's that it's never fun when you put on the shoes of others. I never knew what dads and moms felt when their sons got on a plane at my orders, until my son called me up in August, 2009, and said, "Dad, I am deploying to Iraq." Now I know what it feels like and it hurts. So God bless all you parents, sisters, brothers, wives, husbands and, of course, God bless all our former and present service members.

Just the other day I told Cathy, "Honey, I need to burn all these pairs of shoes."

She said, "You don't have any extra shoes. Every six months you give away half your stuff whether you need it or not. What shoes are you referring to?"

I replied, "The shoes that others have never put on. I need a new pair of shoes with no lessons." I was thinking of suicide, PTS battles, sleeping with a sleep apnea machine, and sending my son to war.

She replied, "No you don't. Those lessons have made you who you are; I wouldn't have you any other way. Look at how many folks you have helped." I was speechless.

CHAPTER 23

Continuing my Fight to Help Soldiers

I thought about the last few years since I had curtailed the exhaustive, sapping speech circuit. I had not lessened my fight to help Soldiers and destroy the stigma which hinders them from getting vital help quickly. During the July 1-4 holiday in 2010, I partnered with TUI University and the USO to pass out 1000 free copies of my book, *Changing the Military Culture of Silence*, to America's troops deploying to Iraq and Afghanistan at Hartsfield Airport in Atlanta. This was part of my mission to break down stereotypes associated with the illness and to educate Soldiers coming back from and going to the war zone. A team of volunteers and I had held four Wounded Warrior Horsemanship events for approximately 3000 Soldiers, veterans, and their families at Fort Benning, GA. We had developed, tested and revised the Army's first ever Goal Setting APP, which in itself was recognized by the former Commander of the Maneuver Center of Excellence as "ground breaking." In November, 2012, I was selected to be the liaison for the development of a partnership with Emory University, Callaway Gardens and Fort Benning to create an environment in which Soldiers returning from Iraq or Afghanistan can come to a 10-day strong bonds type program to educate themselves about being successful in life. (I've been a little bit bored with the email, and I am ready to move on. After spending a lot of time relaxing with my family and working on my tan as often as possible, I must admit that a little structure never hurt anyone!)

In 2012, approximately 2000 Soldiers, veterans, and their families participated in the two Wounded Warrior Horsemanship Events which are held semi-annually at Ft. Benning, Georgia. This was the biggest accomplishment of the Warrior Outreach, Inc. team since I had founded The Wounded Warrior Horsemanship Program in 2008. The organization was converted to *Warrior Outreach Inc.* (a Georgia Non-Profit Organization) in 2012. The mission of Warrior Outreach Inc. is to provide the opportunity for Soldiers and veterans from all of America's conflicts to come with their families to connect with horses and receive group-level equine assistance training. We strive to give OIF (Operation Iraqi Freedom) and OEF (Operation Enduring Freedom-Afghanistan) and all veterans the confidence to achieve long term individual and family success. We are staffed entirely by volunteers and are privately funded by donations. *One hundred per cent* of all contributions goes to providing support to those who need it the most. We are totally independent of, and not affiliated with, any other horsemanship program.

In December, 2012, a host of volunteers met to discuss what the year 2013 could bring to this wonderful organization whose sole commitment is to give back to others in every possible way. We held our first Annual SFC Fred H Roberts Memorial Golf Scramble at Woodland Hills where we raised over $3000 for the program. We scheduled the two 2013 Horsemanship events on April 6 and October 5 and two Golf Scrambles on June 15 and December 8 to raise badly needed donations. The association this year will be caring for horses daily, thereby providing more opportunities for horsemanship training. In addition, they will be assisting veterans in repairing broken household items which some veterans, because of their ages or lack of skills, might not be able to repair. Finally, Warrior Outreach planned and opened a beautiful facility on April 5, where veterans, Soldiers, and their families can come to relax, enjoy some southern hospitality, learn basic horsemanship skills, and do some trail riding. We have been blessed by many local and national sponsors who continue to donate to our organization. We appreciate their continued contributions.

CHAPTER 24

Helping One Other Person

Each day for months I have read the Pentagon report that gives a brief summary of Soldiers who have died from vehicle accidents, because of poor health, or by their own hands

It happens almost daily—a Soldier shoots himself, hangs himself, or even takes another life before taking his own. It reminds me of that moment when my world was caving in on me. I can still see the gun in my hand, ready to end it all. I work hard every day to make those thoughts disappear. Working even harder to help others provides me with structure and prevents me from focusing on the negatives of life. I did not pull that trigger. I have been given the gift of life; what I choose to do with it is solely my own responsibility. I won't lose sight of that any time soon. I would like to ask something of you who are reading this book. Pledge to help one other person during your lifetime, in memory of those who sacrificed everything for our country. Yes, it sounds like an easy task, but it's not, because some folks don't want help. Those are the ones I want to help the most. When you help just one person, it is like eating a Krystal hamburger—you cannot eat just one.

CHAPTER 25

A Powerful Story of Success

I recently received an email from Retired Army Colonel Mark Gerner. A West Point graduate, he had been my Battalion Commander from 1990-92. Presently, he is a volunteer Wounded Warrior Mentor for the West Point Society of DC. Trained through seminars, these volunteers patiently counsel our Soldiers who need the care of nurses, life coaches, and listeners. He, as I do, emphasizes the importance of "TLC" in the care of our warriors who are in great physical and mental pain. Many suffer from too much exposure to war, which can be a result of constant rotating. Mark has a message to retirees, a message that urges them to realize that Soldiers, like all of us, do not heal in predictable time periods and, therefore, will certainly need some help. The stigma attached to such need has gone on far too long.

There are definite applications by well-intentioned volunteer and non-profit associations and individuals, but Mark observes that the array of such groups is now very large and does not present a simple and clear choice for the recently wounded, ill, or injured, whose conditions are as varied as anyone could imagine. He believes, as I do, that the only effective care is that which is tailored to an individual plan. We agree that the Army's investment in Warrior Transition organizations and many other systems is nothing short of revolutionary, but the key is not the organization. We both believe that the key is the ability of the wounded Soldier to individually face a combination of physical pain along with complex wounds, as well as other conditions. Such circumstances almost always render the trail much longer and steeper than most of us would expect. The first step for the volunteer, Mark advises, is to listen thoroughly and critically, as a problem solver, without comparisons to other wars, other times, or other people we all know. He recommends taking the Soldiers at their face value and their word. Mark believes that if the volunteer takes this approach, then hopefully the military and Veterans Administration can find ways to effectively expand their professional services to the same end.

Mark heard from a Soldier whom he has been mentoring. His story is warm and encouraging. It enforces the idea that we can help—it does work! This is how Mark, through email, introduced me to the story of Phil Paunescu:

"Phil is a Soldier whom I have been mentoring for the past four years. Having seen several other Soldiers wounded under some confusing conditions, Phil, himself, was wounded while on patrol in Afghanistan in May, 2009. Among his many complex injuries were a shattered heel and TBI. His platoon leader, who was on the mounted patrol that day, had exited the vehicle minutes before the driver, the medic, and Phil hit the I.E.D. In July, 2009, Phil's company commander was killed in action.

"His infantry company, Co. B, 1-4 IN, had deployed from Germany, not as a brigade, but as an individual company whose basic duties were to provide route security. I have spent many hours just listening to this bright young man's assessment of the operations he faced and how he and his platoon members learned, over time, how to act tactically. In October, 2009, after mentoring, tracking, and helping him as much as I could, we managed to move him from Walter Reed to Boca Raton, FL, so he could be near his mother. That meant departing the Warrior Training Unit he was in and moving to a community-based WTU. It was from there that we found a way to get to a Reserve Component organization, because he was an active duty Soldier with no assignment on a day-to-day basis. That is an important matter, because day-to-day duty has a lot to do with one's self-worth. Phil went through just about every wicket and check point of the system, including changed policies by DOD and DA that suspended his Physical Evaluation Board and his Medical Evaluation Board! He also went through a series of pain management and prescription conflicts. Most importantly, as you will realize from his note to me and some others, he went through a period of self-assessment that appears to have placed him on course.

"I told him on the phone one Saturday that the act of listening, while also taking actions in his interest, is perhaps what makes his story so important. The other point that is obvious to me is that this journey takes time, and during that time, people have many more valleys than they do peaks and successes. So, after four years of our relationship, Phil gave me specific permission to pass on his short email. I asked him for his permission to send it to interested people who may benefit in some way from knowing about Phil Paunescu, not only as a 'wounded warrior,' but as a Soldier. I told him that in my opinion our relationship continues, and it has been a privilege to be invited by him to help in ways he may never have understood before we met.

"Phil's case from date of injury to discharge took three years and four months; that should not have been necessary, even under current staffing and funding levels. In my view, the complexity of conditions that both DA and VA engage in for Soldiers such as Phil has outpaced the knowledge of many in the system. The good news is that as he received his final determination, he received it from both the Army and VA together, in writing, and they were in fact coordinated.

"The message for those of us who engage in support and help with such matters is that time, attention, and constant checking to ensure that we are listening are of utmost importance. We must be listening not only to the system, the various chains of command and chains of support, but *listening to the Soldier*. With that introduction, here is Phil's email."

I want to take a moment to thank my friends and family for helping me, putting up with me, mentoring me, and being there for me when I needed someone to talk to. I feel as if 2013 has been a year that's impacted me in several ways. Without a doubt, it's been an emotional rollercoaster! I've been in "transition" since 2009, the year I deployed to Afghanistan and lost my personal battles. I knew war would be a mental, physical, and emotional challenge, but I never thought I'd lose the battle on all three fronts. Most of you who know me, know that I've always been up for a challenge. I joined at the age of 24, considered relatively late in the military world. Dropping out of college, quitting my job, and leaving friends, family, and a perfectly safe environment to join the infantry made little or no sense to anyone. Unless you are active military or a veteran, you'll probably never understand why I did those things. I know in my heart that if I had not had my little "fender bender" on May 10, 2009, I'd still be in and probably would be making the Army my career. I loved it that much, and I don't regret anything I've seen or done. I never speak about it, and the most you'll hear me say is, "I wish I were still there." I think about it every day, and I won't stop until the very last Soldier has returned home from that forsaken place. I lost a lot while I was deployed. It's not every summer that a guy loses his faith, his fiancée, and his athletic abilities. All that in just a few months! However, I feel that by the grace of God and with the help of you guys, I've come full circle. I want to thank and commend each and every one of you personally, and when I have the opportunity, I will do just that. Every one of you that I am tagging below has played a role in my life at one point or another. Some of you have known me since I was a teenager, and others have known me for a short time. Regardless of the length of our relationships, each of you has made a real, positive impact on my life. Things are starting to make more sense now. I understand more clearly why I'm still here, how I should live my life from now on, and how I should treat others. I love my veterans, and I want to help them in any way I can. I want to show people who have physical or mental disorders that they too can fight the fight, as long as they keep a positive attitude and the will to try. I know firsthand that doing so is, without a doubt, much easier said than done. When a handful of friends noticed a positive change in me lately, they asked me what had happened and how I had fostered the change.

My only answer is, "When you hit rock bottom, and you are at a personal crossroads, it's the decisions you make at that point that will lead you to a better you or to the mistakes that, unfortunately, too many veterans and civilians with PTSD and TBI make on a daily basis."

Again, I want to thank you guys for your support and understanding. I also want to apologize to those I've hurt on the way. I know now that what happens to us is only a fraction of life. The main part of life is how we react to what happens. Thank you for your time, support, and love. You have done great things for a veteran in transition, one that can finally close a chapter, at least to a certain degree. I don't think that it would have been possible without you and the prayers. I will return the favor and keep all of you in my prayers. Thank you.

Phil

No one like Phil should ever be chained by stigma. Take the time, pay the attention, listen well, pray sincerely, and break those chains.

EPILOGUE

The NCO Creed

"No one is more professional than I. I am a Noncommissioned Officer, a leader of Soldiers. As a Noncommissioned Officer, I realize that I am a member of a time honored corps, which is known as 'The Backbone of the Army.' I am proud of the Corps of Noncommissioned Officers and will at all times conduct myself so as to bring credit upon the Corps, the Military Service and my country, regardless of the situation in which I find myself. I will not use my grade or position to attain pleasure, profit, or personal safety.

Competence is my watchword. My two basic responsibilities will always be uppermost in my mind—accomplishment of my mission and the welfare of my Soldiers. I will strive to remain technically and tactically proficient. I am aware of my role as a Noncommissioned Officer. I will fulfill my responsibilities inherent in that role. All Soldiers are entitled to outstanding leadership; I will provide that leadership. I know my Soldiers and I will always place their needs above my own. I will communicate consistently with my Soldiers and never leave them uninformed. I will be fair and impartial when recommending both rewards and punishment.

Officers of my unit will have maximum time to accomplish their duties; they will not have to accomplish mine. I will earn their respect and confidence as well as that of my Soldiers. I will be loyal to those with whom I serve; seniors, peers, and subordinates alike. I will exercise initiative by taking appropriate action in the absence of orders. I will not compromise my integrity, nor my moral courage. I will not forget, nor will I allow my comrades to forget that we are professionals, Noncommissioned Officers, leaders!"

Command Sergeant Major (Retired) Samuel Marvin Rhodes asked me for my thoughts concerning this publication. I was honored, yet challenged, by how I could offer any contribution for such a leader's work that would be worthy of inclusion. The NCO Creed, as printed above, came to mind as I thought about this Soldier and friend.

I met CSM Rhodes when he was Sergeant First Class (SFC) Rhodes, the Operations Noncommissioned Officer in Charge (NCOIC) of the 1st Battalion, 64th Armored Regiment (Desert Rogues), 2nd Brigade, 24th Infantry Division (Victory Division) at Fort Stewart, Georgia. Having just been assigned to 1-64AR as the Operations/Training/Plans Officer, or S3, I quickly learned that he was my "go-to" man for getting things done.

SFC Rhodes ran a very squared-away S3 shop. I liked to think it was mine, but it was really his. Actually, it was ours together. We developed a very good relationship in which we communicated well. We still bumped heads and didn't always agree on things, but we worked it out and collaborated on the way ahead. He made things happen. I didn't have to micro-manage things, just give general direction and guidance and step out of the way. He did the rest. Whether it was setting up a Command and Control (C2) system for rotating out Command Posts (CPs) during gunneries, compiling a very complex packet of training plans for a pending deployment to Kuwait, developing a briefing plan and sequence for visiting VIPs, producing a Red-Cycle Operations Plan from A to Z, developing a Family Readiness Group program for our S3 shop Soldiers and their families, or running a rail-head operation for load-out operations, he made it happen.

SFC Rhodes was a strong runner, and so was I. One day, we decided to see who could go longer, faster. Mind you, this was Ft Stewart, where it's always hot and muggy, or at least very warm. Both of us were in very good shape. We took off running one morning to see who could out-do whom, moving out past the rail-head site and through some wood lines. We pretty much tied each other, but it was a good competition. As was typical of a Fort Stewart PT session, we were ringing wet when we were done. It wasn't until I was training Cadets later in my career that I ever ran so hard against another Soldier. I gained great reassurance knowing SFC Rhodes possessed the qualities of endurance and determination.

Later, after he had completed the NCO Battle Staff School at Ft Bliss, he shared with me his frustration with some of his fellow NCOs who could not run at the same pace or distance at which he had performed out there. It wasn't a matter of arrogance; it was a matter of professional drive and expectation. I came to realize that his very high performance standards would continue to define the units which he would lead.

This very driven professional also had a great sense of humor, an attribute which is so important in leading Soldiers. We often found ourselves laughing at his very dry, biting wit. He could find humor in the most unlikely of situations. There was a Temporary Duty (TDY) trip several of us made from our battalion to work with some Georgia National Guard (NG) units one weekend. SFC Rhodes and I were in charge of this effort. Without regurgitating all the details, I must say that when I finally arrived at the hotel where we were bunking for the weekend, he had already arranged with the hotel staff to sabotage my hotel room with banners and other silly paraphernalia, to engage me in very humorous and candid conversation upon check-in, and to ensure I received no less than half a dozen phone calls from the desk staff, throughout the night, to inquire whether or not "everything was okay" with my room. Yes, going TDY with him was quite the experience!

The Battalion / Task Force (TF) deployed to Kuwait that spring for Operation Intrinsic Action. This was a Central Command (CENTCOM) Deployment/Readiness/Training operation that required 1500 Soldiers to deploy, draw pre-positioned stocks of equipment, move to the Kuwaiti desert and immediately start training with the Kuwaiti 115th Armor Brigade. It was designed to test and exercise our ability to quickly move out in the event that Iraq ever posed a significant threat again. This was 1996, after the first Gulf War and before Operation Iraqi Freedom (OIF). The TF did well—very well, in fact. So much of that success was due to how well SFC Rhodes had prepared the S3 shop and the TF for our mission with comprehensive training plans, equipment requirements/demands, ammunition forecasts, and range requirements, and how well our own S3 shop personnel and equipment were prepared. The TF remained in the desert through August, conducting Level-I gunnery for our two armor companies and two infantry companies. It was a great experience.

We stayed in touch over the years after sharing time at Stewart. SFC Rhodes became a First Sergeant (1SG) and later Sergeant Major (SGM), and eventually a Command Sergeant Major. He continued to excel in every task assigned and took on more and more responsibilities. As Operation Enduring Freedom (OEF) and OIF continued, SGM Rhodes found himself deploying not once, not twice, but three times to Iraq—first with the 2nd ACR as the Regimental Operations Sergeant Major, later with the 3rd Army, and finally as the Command Sergeant Major 2nd Squadron, 11th ACR . We stayed in touch through occasional emails and Christmas cards.

CSM Rhodes carried the hidden wounds of three combat tours inside him when he returned to Fort Benning to serve as the CSM of the Infantry School Training Brigade. After much soul-searching and anguish, he finally realized and publicly acknowledged that he suffered from Post-Traumatic Stress Disorder (PTSD). In doing so, he realized that part of his healing needed to include a concerted effort on his part to "give back" to the extended family he had come to know so very well—his fellow Soldiers and their families—and to confront the issues plaguing him.

To talk with Sergeant Major, to hear the tone of his voice when he shares with you the driving need that fills his heart to do something affirming so that others can protect themselves against the pains of PTSD, or if they already are suffering, to encourage seeking help and support, is to hear the most solemn and moving expression of compassion one can imagine. There is no self-serving agenda or effort to seek the spotlight. His desire to "give back" is as genuine and as sincere a calling as your or my need to breathe. It has truly come to define his life. His productivity and energies are all centered on finding new ways to help others, while maintaining the momentum he has already garnered with so many. Just a few years ago, my wife and I traveled to Georgia to join him and his wife, Cathy, to celebrate his 50th birthday. It was a wonderful, food-filled event. Their beautiful home was full of family, friends and so many people who had come to know CSM over the years. There were many things that caught my attention that evening in his home, but one of the most striking occurred when he and a few friends were looking at the certificates for some of his medals. In each instance, when he focused on a particular award, CSM Rhodes would mention the name of one or two close friends with whom he had worked during that particular period. Without fail, when discussing each award, he mentioned someone else who had been there, too, and, in his own words, had done even more.

Several years later, my wife and I ventured down to Benning again to attend our son's graduation from Airborne School. CSM and Cathy hosted us at their home once again. We were joined by our son's girlfriend who wanted to see the ceremony. CSM made her feel just like family, kidding with her and cracking jokes, but ensuring she knew just how special the guests in their home were treated. It was a great trip with some very proud moments.

During the summer of 2013, our son, a lieutenant at Fort Polk, was about to deploy to Afghanistan. It's a different feeling when it's one of your very own children. We were at Polk, finishing breakfast with our son after a three-day visit and about to start the long drive back to Ohio, when my cell phone rang. It was CSM. Somehow he knew what was going on. We spoke briefly and then he asked if "that young lieutenant" was around and if he could speak with him. Brian knew CSM, and he knew who he was in our lives. I handed our son my phone.

Brian laughed a bit. Once again that sense of humor had come through. CSM asked Brian if he had received the book he had sent him, and Brian acknowledged that he had and that he was going to read it. (It was a personally autographed copy of CSM's first book.) They continued to talk as Brian walked out of the restaurant into the Louisiana sunshine. He came back in shortly and handed me the phone. CSM asked me to give my bride a hug from him and Cathy and to be careful driving back to Ohio. He closed by saying, "That's a good, young man, your son." Yes, he is indeed.

Regardless of where I find myself, or what I may be doing, CSM Sam Rhodes will know when and how to reach out to me. He knows when I need a little pep-talk, a slice of humor, or just a chance to unload with someone who understands. And he knows when I need advice, or just someone to listen.

As I write these words, which have gone on far longer than I intended, I think about the Warrior Outreach initiatives Sam has championed, ranging from equestrian gatherings that have now expanded to more than a thousand participating Soldiers, families and veterans, to the overseeing of building a home for a Vietnam veteran's widow who literally had nothing left of her original domain. She hadn't asked for any help, but somehow found herself befriended by CSM and his team. I think about his cell phone, which, even when he and Cathy are sitting on our back deck in Cincinnati, Ohio, drinking a cold one and enjoying dinner, never stops ringing. The calls are from people needing guidance for any untold number of projects he is overseeing, or from an old friend who just needs a minute to talk, to share, and to have someone listen.

Many of us "grew up" in the Army, hoping to make a difference, hoping to lead well, and hoping to touch peoples' lives in a positive and meaningful way. In my book, the most successful among us, having made the greatest impact and having touched the most lives, is a wonderful and caring gentleman, whose energy, compassion, and commitment to others know no bounds. He is a man who will always be my friend—Command Sergeant Major (Retired) Sam Rhodes.

I hope you have enjoyed reading Sam's book. Share it with those you love.

Philip R. Tilly
Lieutenant Colonel
United States Army (Retired)

Samuel M Rhodes, Cathy Rhodes, and General George W. Casey

About the Author

Samuel M. Rhodes
Command Sergeant Major
United States Army (Retired)

Command Sergeant Major (Retired) Samuel M. Rhodes retired from the Army in January, 2009, after 29 years of service, including three tours in Iraq. During his Army career, he was awarded the Combat Infantry Badge, the Bronze Star 1st Oak Leaf, the Legion of Merit, and seven Meritorious Service Medals. Diagnosed with Post Traumatic Stress Disorder (PTSD) in 2005, he was one of the first senior leaders in the military to openly state that he had issues with mental health, as a result of his war experiences. While dealing with his own struggles, Mr. Rhodes has worked tirelessly to encourage Soldiers and veterans to address their psychological problems and seek immediate help for them.

His relentless commitment to his fellow warriors and their families has not only saved lives, but has helped them and society to overcome the stigma associated with mental health issues. For his personal courage and outstanding efforts, Mr. Rhodes has received numerous accolades, including those from Chief of Staff of the Army, General George W. Casey, and Sergeant Major of the Army, Kenneth O. Preston. In addition, in 2009, Lockheed Martin presented their Community Service and Global Excellence Award for Building Effective Relationships to Mr. Rhodes, honoring him for the great contributions he had made to the community. Currently, Mr. Rhodes is employed by the Army at Ft. Benning, Georgia, as the Program Manager for Comprehensive Soldier and Family Fitness. He is the founder and CEO of Warrior Outreach, Inc., and the author of *Changing the Military Culture of Silence*. Mr. Rhodes and his wife, Cathy, reside near Columbus, Georgia, and have six children and seven grandchildren.

CPSIA information can be obtained at www.ICGtesting.com
Printed in the USA
LVOW06s2047250214

375137LV00002B/4/P